MINI

MADEIRA

How to download your Free eBook

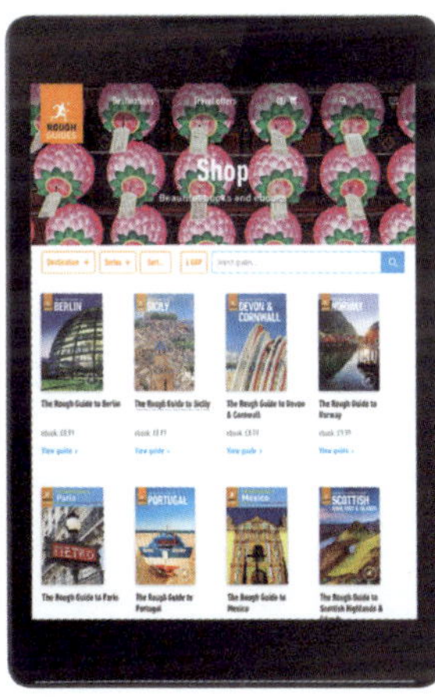

1. Visit **www.roughguides.com/free-ebook** or scan the **QR code** opposite

2. Enter the code **madeira440**

3. Follow the simple step-by-step instructions

For troubleshooting contact: mail@roughguides.com

Samsonite

Contents

Introduction

The Madeira Islands are an archipelago, formed from volcanic eruptions many millions of years ago. A mere speck in the Atlantic Ocean, the main island, Madeira, is thickly draped with vegetation. Massive, rugged mountains peek through the clouds, and micro-climates hover over isolated villages. Spectacular cliffs crash down to the surf below.

Although the islands were known to Roman and Carthaginian sailors 2,000 years ago, Madeira was only settled a few decades before Columbus made his way to America. It became part of the Portuguese empire after fifteenth century navigators claimed it for King João I. But Madeira is nearer to Africa than to Lisbon. It lies 600km (372 miles) off the coast of Morocco and nearly 1,000km (620 miles) southwest of the Portuguese capital.

Apart from Madeira itself, only one other island in the group is inhabited – the arid, much flatter holiday hideaway of Porto Santo. Christopher Columbus visited Porto Santo in the second

WHEN TO GO

Madeira is warmed by the Gulf Stream, which ensures mild, sub-tropical weather. While it's genuinely a year-round destination, the peak months are July and August, when it's warmest, sunniest and calmest. The low season months of November to January are windy, with more than ten times as much rain per month than July, the driest. Even so, in mid-winter, you can expect an average of five hours of sunshine a day. For flowers and hiking, spring and summer are best, with gardens and verges in bloom and the air warm and clear. For sea swimming and other water-sports, July to October is warmest. Most festivals take place between Easter and September, but there are some exceptions to this – Christmas and New Year, for example, are celebrated with gusto, and hotels are often fully booked at this time.

half of the fifteenth century, and married the local governor's granddaughter.

Waterfalls dot the interior

Natural wonders

Few places on earth can rival Madeira's wealth of natural gifts, especially in so small an area. In the countryside, there's an abundance of colourful flowers and trees. Strelizias display their bright orange, beak-like blooms in open fields. Fragrant hydrangeas line walking paths skirting the edges of mountain terraces. Private and public gardens burst with orchids, bougainvillea and jacaranda trees, while orchards and plantations heave with apples, pears, cherries, passion fruit, bananas and avocados.

In the mountains, water streams down from unseen springs: a one-hour walk might take you past half a dozen waterfalls. The cold waters around the island, once prime whaling territory, are now a marine sanctuary for whales, dolphins and seals. And all of this in year-round sub-tropical weather, with a southerly breeze and temperatures that average 22°C (72°F) in the summer and 17°C (63°F) during the winter.

Size and population

Madeira seems much larger than its diminutive size, just 57km (35 miles) long and 22km (13 miles) wide. The terrain is so mountainous that distances are magnified in terms of both time and effort.

Funchal is a major harbour

In the past, this bred insularity: before fast roads were constructed, some villagers never travelled to the capital, Funchal (pronounced 'foon-shall'), let alone to mainland Portugal.

With a history of emigration and return, of welcoming visiting merchants and, during a brief period of occupation, a garrison of British troops, the islanders are a cosmopolitan mix: some have Portuguese or North African ancestry, while others are descended from northern Europeans. Even today, it's common for the young and upwardly mobile to seek opportunities overseas; the most successful return and build sumptuous villas.

The capital city

Funchal, set on Madeira's passenger harbour, is the only city of any note. Hinting at the island's riches, its white houses with tiled roofs are clustered on picturesque hills sloping down to a steep bay.

Almost half of Madeira's 251,000-strong population live and work here, and as a result parts of the city can feel congested at times. Nonetheless, it's a highly strollable capital, with pleasant seafront promenades, a marina, leafy squares, cobbled streets and a high concentration of cafés, restaurants, historic churches and museums. Some visitors spend their entire stay in and around Funchal, where they can choose between the gleaming high-rise hotels of the *zona hoteleira*, the townhouse hotels of the historic centre and the distinguished *quintas* (villas and mansions) of Madeira's peaceful past.

The rural interior

Funchal is a gateway to the rest of the island, whose real charms begin in the hillsides just a few minutes outside town. Spectacular gardens, including the Jardim Botânico and Quinta do Palheiro, are only a short bus, taxi or cable car ride from the capital.

Small-scale agriculture dominates the island's landscape, and employs about a fifth of its people. Depending on the altitude, and whether you are on the warm south coast or the marginally

DESERTAS AND SELVAGENS

As well as the two inhabited islands of Madeira and Porto Santo, the North Atlantic archipelago comprises another five uninhabited islands and numerous minor rocks and reefs. The islands fall into two groups: the Ilhas Desertas (Desert Islands) and the Ilhas Selvagens (Wild or Savage Islands).

The former consists of three islands, the nearest situated 12km (19 miles) southeast of Madeira. These desert islands are far from the Robinson Crusoe idyll: they are barren and inhospitable to the point where, aside from the occasional goat and rabbit, the most notable land creature is a large, venomous black spider.

But the sea life around the islands is a different story. Dolphins and turtles are occasionally spotted, and there is a colony of very rare Mediterranean monk seals. Bird-watchers will relish the opportunity to see shearwaters and petrels. Marine biologists and nature conservationists are the only regular human visitors, for even though excursion boats frequently make trips to these isles in summer, landing is restricted to authorised persons only.

Meanwhile, the two Selvagens Islands, usually known as Grande (Large) and Pequena (Small), are Madeiran only in name. They lie 285km (177 miles) to the south, closer to the Canary Islands than to Madeira. Like the Desertas, they are devoted entirely to nature conservation.

cooler north coast, you will see terraces of bananas, and the vines that produce the grapes for fortified Madeira wine. There are windswept mountain peaks, craggy cliffs and emerald valleys. From strategically situated lookout points *(miradouros)* you can take in these magical panoramas and look down on villages and terraced fields carved out of the mountains.

New roads and tunnels make driving around Madeira faster than before, though the best scenery is reserved for those who follow the hairpin bends of mountain roads and coastal lanes, getting sprayed by waterfalls and constantly stopping to enjoy spectacular vistas. Madeira is even better when explored on foot. The island is heaven for anyone who enjoys being outside, whether your taste tends to gentle walks or hardcore hiking. Madeira's system of irrigation channels, known as *levadas*, carries water down from the mountains on gentle gradients and provides a ready-made system of trails. The canals – more than 2,100km (1,300 miles) of them wrap around the island – have level footpaths running along their entire length. Walkers of all ages and abilities need only find a *levada* to take in some of the finest countryside anywhere. Several of these walks, described later in this book (see page 81), are among the highlights of Madeira.

Ponta de São Lourenço, Madeira's easternmost point

WHAT'S NEW

Madeira's top-flight dining scene has blossomed in recent years. One of Funchal's hottest new restaurants, Desarma, which opened in 2023, clocked up its first Michelin star in 2024, retaining it in 2025. The islands are also stepping up their longstanding commitment to sustainability and environmental protection. In 2023, the World Cetacean Alliance designated Madeira a World Heritage Area, in recognition of its success in protecting an important marine habitat that supports 26 whale and dolphin species, and in 2024 Madeira launched a new three-day event, the Festival da Baleia (Whale Festival), featuring live music and exhibitions. In 2023–24, Madeira was awarded EarthCheck Silver status as a Sustainable Tourism Destination; other recent accolades include Porto Santo being named Europe's Leading Beach Destination in the 2024 World Travel Awards, and Madeira winning World's Best Emerging Golf Destination in the 2024 World Golf Awards.

With such rapturous scenery and a climate that is consistently delightful, perhaps it would be unfair to expect nature to have bestowed miles of perfect sands on the island as well. Madeira has few beaches as such, although most coastal villages have swimming pools and sea access, and Calheta and the bay of Machico have artificial beaches with imported golden sand. But if a chair by the pool just can't compare with waves lapping on sand, you will have to follow in the wake of Columbus and dock on the neighbouring island of Porto Santo. A popular day trip, it has a 9km (5.5 mile) beach running the length of its south coast, and refreshingly few other attractions.

While some surely would find the notion of an island holiday with no beach time an unusual prospect, perhaps it isn't such a tragedy that Madeira's shoreline crashes so violently into the ocean. Lack of sand has kept Madeira from becoming as popular as the Canary Islands, Mallorca or Ibiza, which has helped preserve its environment. Yet tourism is eroding the island in other ways,

Funchal during the Flower Festival

as traditional farming gives way to a tourism economy, as a result leaving the vertiginous hills untended and the picturesque terraces and *levadas* in a state of decline.

Tourism and Madeira

For decades, Madeira attracted a genteel, even anachronistic, form of island tourism. Afternoon tea and a jacket and tie at dinner are still de rigueur at the most elegant hotels. The typical visitor is still older and wealthier than in most holiday destinations, but times have changed

NOTES

Some of the mountain villages of Madeira are so isolated that they did not begin to receive TV signals until the 1980s.

– as they have across Portugal, which is no longer the forgotten backwater of Europe. Funchal's enlarged airport, upgraded road network and increasing numbers of new hotels testify to local travel-industry ambitions.

Today, Madeira is being discovered by younger travellers and digital nomads, who might indulge in the spas and dining that world-class hotels offer, but are just as likely to seek out more modest accommodation up in the mountains and pull on their boots for serious hiking.

Madeirans, like most Portuguese, are a generally quiet and reserved people. Add to this geographical isolation and the difficulties of a harsh, mostly agricultural existence and you might well expect the islanders to be less than welcoming. Instead, you will find friendly people who, in spite of a year-long tourism season, are refreshingly hospitable. They are proud of the scenic beauty, delectable wines and exquisite hand embroidery for which their tiny island has rightly become famous.

SUSTAINABLE TRAVEL

Madeira takes great pride in being certified as a sustainable tourism destination by EarthCheck, an organisation accredited by the World Council for Sustainable Tourism. The archipelago's Sustainability Policy includes working towards decarbonising its transport network, conserving green spaces, replanting trees and promoting low-impact activities such as hiking and cycling. Steps that can help make your visit sustainable include eating at restaurants that specialise in traditional or contemporary Madeiran or Azorean cuisine, using local ingredients, and buying from shops and markets that sell products from local artisans, manufacturers and growers. Other green choices include travelling around the islands by bus, bike, electric car or ferry rather than by petrol car or inter-island plane, and spinning out your stay to reduce your airmiles per day.

1

2

3

10 Things not to miss

4

5

6

1 **MADEIRA'S HILLS AND MOUNTAINS**
Venture out on spectacular scenic walks. See page 66.

2 **ADEGAS DE SÃO FRANCISCO (BLANDY'S WINE LODGE)**
Visit the oldest working wine cellars on Madeira. See page 37.

3 **MONTE**
A hilltop village above Funchal, known for its gardens and exhilarating toboggan rides. See page 49.

4 **JARDIM BOTÂNICO**
Marvel at Madeira's extravagant flowers. See page 47.

5 **PICO DO ARIEIRO**
Drive above the clouds to reach Madeira's second-highest peak. See page 64.

6 **FUNCHAL'S MUSEU DE ARTE SACRA**
Outstanding Flemish paintings enjoy pride of place in this museum. See page 40.

7 **PORTO SANTO**
Relax on gorgeous golden sands on the island that's Madeira's little sister. See page 74.

8 **MADEIRA'S LIDO COMPLEXES AND NATURAL POOLS**
Enjoy an outdoor dip in beautiful surroundings. See page 83.

9 **PALHEIRO COTTAGES**
These traditional thatched cottages are still in use in the Santana region. See page 67.

10 **SÃO VICENTE**
One of Madeira's most attractive villages, with volcanic caves nearby. See page 61.

A perfect tour of Madeira

DAY 1

Funchal at its best. Get your bearings by exploring the historic quarter around the Sé (Cathedral), then split the remainder of the day between the magnificent Quinta das Cruzes and the splendid Adegas de São Francisco (Blandy's Wine Lodge). In the former, check out the antiques and art objects of one of Funchal's grandest mansions, and in the latter, learn about the history of Madeira's fortified wines, followed by a tasting.

DAY 2

Market and Old Town. Still in Funchal, browse the Mercado dos Lavradores, a busy, colourful spectacle, with leather goods, wickerwork, and handicrafts on sale alongside fruit, vegetables and fish. Wander the Old Town, enjoying the lively atmosphere of its cafés, restaurants and galleries.

DAY 3

Cable cars and Monte. Take in the views from the Teleférico do Funchal cable car that zooms up from the Old Town to Monte. Here, explore the lush Jardim Tropical Monte Palace, then ride downhill in a *carro de cesto* (traditional wicker street toboggan). Alternatively, hop in another cable car to glide down to the Jardim Botânico.

DAY 4

Hill gardens. Spend the day exploring the Palheiro Gardens, the most magnificent of Madeira's many splendid green spaces. Draped over a hillside, the estate is a short bus ride from Funchal, and famous for its exotic plants, wild ravine, ancient trees and winter camellias.

DAY 5

Mountain scenery. Take a public bus or an organised tour to the summit of Madeira's third highest mountain, Pico do Arieeiro in the central highlands. It's something of a moonscape, where plunging barren volcanic landscapes glow russet red in the sunlight.

DAY 6

Hidden valley. Next, head to the other-worldly Curral das Freiras, which you can reach via bus, car or organised tour. Encircled by a ring of mountains, it was for a long time barely accessible from the coast. It's an extraordinary sight, with the steep slopes striped with terraces.

DAY 7

São Vicente and Porto Moniz. WIth its delightful church and picturesque setting, the prettiness of São Vicente village is worth the cross-island trip from Funchal. From here, continue northwest to Porto Moniz, home to inviting natural pools, fringed by volcanic rocks.

DAY 8

Madeira's sleepy little sister. Fly or take a boat to Porto Santo island, with its 9km (5.6 miles) of golden beach. Explore lost-in-time villages, a rugged interior and scuba diving sites, or simply snooze on the sandy shore.

Madeira on a budget

DAY 1

Cobbles and churches. After breakfast at your hotel, wander around Funchal's historic centre, admiring its elegant architecture and mosaic-cobbled streets and squares. For a visual and spiritual feast, visit some of the city's sumptuously decorated churches, such as the Sé (Cathedral), with its fabulous Mudéjar-style ceilings, and the Igreja do Colégio on Praça do Município, adorned with frescoes, gilded carvings and ornamental tiles. Mid-morning, pop into a café to fuel up on coffee (espresso shots are a snip at well under two euros) and, at lunchtime, head for Delícia das Sopas, on a lane near the cathedral, for a quick, tasty bowl of classic Madeiran chicken or chunky vegetable soup with salad and bread.

City dip. In the afternoon, visit the Complexo Balnear do Lido for a refreshing open-air swim. You can relax at this popular coastal pool all afternoon for less than €6, but in high season (April to September) it's even cheaper – less than half price – if you wait for the sunset session, which starts two hours before it closes at 7pm.

Poncha and petiscos. Soak up the sights and sounds of Funchal in the early evening, perhaps enjoying a glass of poncha (local punch) and some petiscos (tapas) at one of the historic centre's many bars. Before the end of the day, pack some food and drink for tomorrow morning and set an alarm for an early start.

DAY 2

Heady heights. Rising before dawn, dress in warm layers, grab your supplies and head for Funchal's Teleférico bus stop, starting point for the 6am Horários do Funchal bus to Pico do Areeiro. Travelling via Monte and Poiso, it takes 45 minutes to reach Madeira's third-highest summit, and the fare, payable on the bus, is just €3 each way. Since there are only 31 seats on board, it's a good idea to reserve one in advance, by phone (tel: 291 705 555), two to seven days beforehand. Once at the top, you have 5.5 hours to enjoy the strikingly rugged and barren mountain scenery before the return bus leaves at 12.15pm – enough time to walk at least part of the iconic PR1 hiking trail to the highest peak, Pico Ruivo, 7km away. The trail fee is €3.

Coastal cool. Back in Funchal's Old Town, grab a healthy lunch at Art Food Corner, then take in some of the district's latest street art. Later, enjoy a gentle stroll along the pleasant seafront and relax in Parque de Santa Catarina before heading west into the Hotel Zone for happy hour.

Gourmet Madeira

DAY 1

Pequeno almoço. If your hotel lays on a sumptuous breakfast, enjoy, but try to be selective: you have three full days of temptation ahead. For something distinctively Madeiran, choose bolo do caco (stone-baked bread made from wheat and sweet potato flour), tropical fruit and a galão (espresso with warm foamy milk).

Funchal culinary tour. Taste your way around town on a guided food and drink tour. Visiting selected market stalls, bakeries, cheese shops and poncha bars, you'll receive a crash course in Madeira's gastronomic heritage. Round off your excursion with an in-depth tour of the Adegas de São Francisco (Blandy's Wine Lodge), where you can discover the fascinating cultural history of Madeira wine and taste its varieties: Sercial, Malvasia, Verdelho and Boal.

Desarma. In the evening, make your way to The Views Baía Hotel for dinner. True to its name, this sleek, modern hotel has stunning views over Funchal Bay. Its restaurant, Desarma, made waves when it launched in 2023, and has won a Michelin star. Madeiran chef Octávio Freitas creates complex, visually arresting dishes that combine diverse flavours in original ways.

DAY 2

Lazy morning in Funchal. After breakfast, head back to Funchal's superb Mercado dos Lavradores to browse its many fruit, fish and confectionery stalls at leisure. Sip a speciality coffee on the rooftop at Three House, near the market, then stroll into the cathedral quarter and grab a pavement table for an early lunch at Informal, where the beautifully conceived set menu changes every week.

Wine and fruit tour. Jump into a taxi or minibus for a bespoke tour of the vineyards and orchards of Estreito de Câmara de Lobos, Ponta do Sol, São Vicente and Seixal. At BAM, the Madeira Banana Museum, you can learn about this iconic fruit and taste banana beer, while the Museum of Wine and the Vine in Arco de São Jorge offers insights into local wine-making. End the day with dinner at Quinta do Furão, a delightful vineyard restaurant.

DAY 3

Contemporary café. Boost your caffeine intake with a mid-morning artisan coffee at Arbor, an appealing café opposite Parque de Santa Catarina. The garden setting is so appealing that you may want to linger for a light and healthy brunch or lunch. In the afternoon, enjoy a stroll, swim or sport session, to work up an appetite for tonight's feast.

Il Gallo D'Or. Boasting two Michelin stars, the elegant fine-dining restaurant at The Cliff Bay hotel is nothing short of exceptional. Chef Benoît Sinthon's sophisticated tasting menus demonstrate his flair for selecting the very best ingredients from Madeira's waters, mountains and gardens, and showcase his impeccable culinary technique.

History

As befits a lush, subtropical island stranded in the ocean, Madeira's origins are shrouded in fanciful legend. Some claim that the archipelago is all that remains of Plato's lost Atlantis, or that it is part of a landmass that once fused the continents of Europe and America. Recorded history begins in relatively recent times; in the early fifteenth century, just as the golden age of Portuguese discovery was erupting. Under the direction of Henry the Navigator (Henrique o Navegador), caravels set out from the Algarve, in southern Portugal, in search of foreign lands, fame and wealth. João Gonçalves Zarco, sailing in the service of Prince Henry, made the first of many famous Portuguese discoveries: in 1418 he happened upon a small volcanic archipelago 1,000km (620 miles) from Lisbon.

THE FIRST MAN ON MADEIRA?

Some say that the first man to set foot on the island was not the Portuguese adventurer João Gonçalves Zarco but a fourteenth-century Englishman named Robert Machim (sometimes written as Machin).

One version of the story is that Machim was a knight at the court of Edward III and sought to marry above his station, to a girl named Anne d'Arfet (or Anne of Hertford). The determined young lovers boarded a ship bound for France, which was thrown severely off course. The pair ended up shipwrecked on Madeira. Anne died of exposure soon afterwards, and Machim buried her by the bay where they had come ashore. When Machim died (it is said of a broken heart), the surviving crew buried him alongside her. The crew, who lived to recount the tragic tale, eventually escaped the island on a log raft.

Zarco, who is much more widely credited with the discovery of Madeira, was aware of the legend. He is said to have found the tThe couple's resting place is said to be beneath the Capela dos Milagres on the eastern side of Machico Bay (see page 72).

Perhaps Zarco knew precisely where he was heading, having learned of the existence of Madeira from a Castilian source. After all, the waters of the Canary Islands, only 445km (275 miles) to the south, had supported busy shipping lanes for very nearly a century, and Genovese maps from the mid-fourteenth century depict both Madeira and Porto Santo.

Henry the Navigator

More likely, Zarco was heading for Guinea and storms forced him onto the beach of Porto Santo. If so, then he was fortunate, for he managed to land on the only large, sandy beach for hundreds of miles around.

Portugal's first colony

In 1419, Zarco returned to claim the larger island he had seen from Porto Santo, and with him went Tristão Vaz Teixeira and Bartolomeu Perestrelo. They officially became the first men to set foot on the heavily forested island, naming it *Ilha da Madeira* – Island of Timber.

The Portuguese Crown, delighted with its first important discovery, embarked on a programme of colonisation. In 1425, King João I pronounced Madeira an official province of Portugal, and presented it as a gift to Prince Henry (Infante Dom Henrique). He, in turn, confirmed the land ownership rights to Zarco and Teixeira, while Perestrelo was awarded Porto Santo.

NOTES

It seems certain that Madeira had never been inhabited before the Portuguese arrived in the fifteenth century. The first settlers found no Stone Age natives, as the Spanish had found in the Canary Islands, and no mysterious monuments to the past, as in the Balearics.

Occupation of Madeira began in the early 1420s as a small-scale project: colonists arrived with only as much as they could carry from Portugal. They found plenty of water pouring down from the mountains, and more timber than anyone knew what to do with. They set about clearing the land for agriculture, setting fire to tracts of forest. Legend says that a great fire burned for seven years on the island.

Energetic agriculture

The fire provided the soil with a rich ash fertiliser, which complemented the luxuriant growing conditions of tropical sun and plentiful water. The Portuguese saw valuable economic opportunity in their new possession and sent for Malvasia grapes from Crete and sugar cane from Sicily in an effort to seed the island's first cash crops. The project was not a simple one. Colonists had to find enough level ground to grow crops on, and then solve the issue of irrigating them. Probably with the assistance of slaves from the Canary Islands, and without machinery, they carved flat surfaces out of the steep slopes, building the terraces that are seen today.

The problem of watering crops was solved by the irrigation system known as *levadas* – simply designed water channels that wound down from water sources on the verdant mountain tops. The *levadas* were largely built by enslaved labourers, whose primary employment was on sugar plantations. Madeirans traded sugar, the era's dominant luxury item, with Venice and Flanders, and proved skilful in the art of wine-making. The island's burgeoning economic significance propelled population growth, and by the middle of the fifteenth century Madeira was home to some 800 families. A census in 1514 recorded 5,000 inhabitants, not including enslaved people.

In 1478, Madeira welcomed a visitor who would greatly assist the island's future wine trade. Christopher Columbus, not yet a sailor of any renown, sailed to Madeira on an assignment to buy sugar cane. His sojourn was unsuccessful, as money failed to arrive for part of the shipment. Yet Columbus (Cristóvão Colombo in Portuguese) returned six years later, by which time evidence suggests he had become an experienced sugar merchant. His later discovery of the New World brought prosperity to the Madeiran economy: the island's strategic location on the great East–West trading route meant that ships anchored and took on food, water and the valuable trading commodity of Madeira wine.

Columbus married Dona Filipa Moniz Perestrelo, who was the granddaughter of Porto Santo's first governor, and who fathered a son on the island. Even today, there are people on Porto Santo who will tell you that it was during the time he spent there that Columbus learned navigation techniques, and also found the inspiration to undertake his voyage which took place in 1492. His house on Porto Santo is now a museum.

Columbus arrived as a sugar trader and became a resident

Plundered by pirates

From early in the sixteenth century, Madeira became the target of pirate attacks. Noticing the island's wealth and repository of supplies, buccaneers from Morocco, Algeria and France invaded coastal settlements, leaving a trail of death and destruction. In 1566, Madeira suffered its worst disaster when the French pirate Bertrand de Montluc sailed into Funchal harbour with his 11-galleon armada and 1,300 men. He unleashed a 16-day reign of terror which left 300 Madeirans dead and sugar stocks plundered.

As a result, Porto Santo, which had also been scourged by these villains of the seas, built hilltop beacons to serve as early-warning systems.

On the mainland, in 1580, Felipe II of Spain proclaimed himself king of Portugal and marched his armies across the border. For the next 60 years, Madeira was a Spanish territory.

At the end of the sixteenth century, Madeira surrendered its domination of the sugar-cane industry to another, much larger, Portuguese colony: Brazil. Sugar cane had taken a hefty toll on the Madeiran soil and the exhausted plantation soils were supplanted by less demanding grape vines.

NOTES

The notorious English pirate Captain Kidd was hanged in London after terrorising the high seas for almost a decade – but the loot he amassed was never found. Legend has it that it's buried somewhere on the Ilhas Desertas, southeast of Madeira, although all searches so far have been fruitless.

Madeira and Britain

Britain's political and economic connections to Madeira can be traced to the seventeenth century. In 1662, Charles II married Portugal's Catherine of Bragança, and a provision written into the bride's dowry granted special favours to British settlers on Madeira. A new regulation

Photograph of Madeira harbour, taken in 1896

made Madeira wine the only wine that could be exported directly to the British possessions in the Western hemisphere. Such trading rights attracted more Britons to the island, who founded dynastic families, some of whom still constitute the island's economic elite. Wine profits were huge, and by 1800 exports had reached 9-million bottles per year. Many of the grand *quintas* (villas) that still dot the island today were built for winemakers.

British troops arrived on the island in 1801 to protect against possible invasion by the French, but they were withdrawn following the Treaty of Amiens in 1802. In 1807, the treaty was put in jeopardy and the troops returned, remaining until 1814. After the fall of Napoleon, many of the garrison remained and settled permanently on the island.

On Madeira, the second half of the nineteenth century was

The seaplane service from England

plagued by natural disaster. In 1852, the island's precious vines were blighted by mildew, wiping out an estimated 90 percent of the total crop. Just four years later, cholera claimed the lives of up to 7,000 Madeirans, and in 1872–3 the dreaded phylloxera louse destroyed the remainder of the vineyards. Potato and sugar crops were also badly affected.

Portugal took up arms during World War I, siding with the British and French. Madeira's strategic position for Atlantic shipping did not escape the notice of the German High Command, and in 1916 a German submarine bombarded Funchal harbour and sank three French ships.

Modern times

As mainland Portugal lurched into a political and economic crisis that would bring down the country's republican government, Madeira was busy developing its tourist trade: the island had been a sought-after destination since the mid-nineteenth century, attracting wealthy sun-lovers, minor royalty and aristocrats. The celebrated Reid's Hotel opened its doors in 1890, and a seaplane service started operating from Southampton in 1921. Madeira gained further cachet when the last of the Austro-Hungarian emperors, Karl I of Austria, chose Madeira as his home in exile after World War I. He died here in 1922 and his last resting place, in

Monte's Nossa Senhora church, now receives a stream of pilgrims, following his beatification by Pope John Paul II in 2004.

In 1932, Portugal gained a new ruler, Dr António Salazar. His success at controlling inflation and reducing national debt made him a popular hero, but under the new ultra-conservative constitution of 1933 he effectively became dictator for life. Following a bloodless military coup in 1974, Salazar's successor, Dr Marcelo Caetano, was overthrown and free elections were held. Two years later, Madeira was granted the status of Autonomous Political Region. A new island parliament would henceforth deal with all issues directly affecting Madeira, except defence, foreign affairs and tax, and for the first time Madeira was allowed to elect five members to the parliament in Lisbon.

In 1986, Portugal joined the EEC (now the European Union). Generous funding from the EU has been invested in the island's fishing industry and infrastructure, such as roads, tunnels, marinas, leisure complexes and the airport. When the EU money dried up, President Alberto João Jardim turned to private investors to continue the building boom and in 2012, the tiny island found itself €6

CELEBRATED STOPOVERS

Madeira, with its long tradition of hospitality, has welcomed many notable voyagers, including, in 1815, the defeated Napoleon Bonaparte. En route to exile on St Helena in the South Atlantic, Napoleon's ship anchored to take on supplies. The only visitor allowed aboard was the British consul, who graciously presented Britain's old enemy with bottles of vintage Madeira wine to help wile away his confinement. Napoleon responded with gold coins. History almost repeated itself after the 1974 coup, when the deposed Portuguese leaders, ex-President Tomás and Prime Minister Caetano, stopped at Madeira en route to exile in Brazil. This time the defeated party was allowed ashore, but they were locked up in the São Lourenço fortress.

billion in debt. In 2015, Madeira elected a new president, Miguel Abuquerque (Social Democratic Party).

In 2016, the island was ravaged by wildfires that caused widespread devastation. Following the worst summer heatwave in history, flames destroyed 22 percent of Funchal. Hundreds were forced to abandon their homes and three people were killed. Another season of serious wildfires hit Madeira in 2024.

Between 2020 and 2021, Madeira's tourism industry stalled due to measures taken to contain Covid-19. Post-pandemic, the island renewed its focus on sustainability, nature, outdoor activities, wellness, food and wine, and visitor numbers gradually bounced back. Certified as a Sustainable Tourism Destination by Earthcheck in 2023, Madeira wins new tourism industry awards every year.

Funchal's goverment office

Chronology

1351 A Genoese map depicts Madeira for the first time.

1418 Portuguese explorers discover Porto Santo.

1425 Madeira becomes a province of Portugal; sugar cultivation begins, followed by grapes and grain.

1478 Christopher Columbus briefly settles on the island.

1480 Settlers arrive from Europe, including merchants who invest in the sugar plantations and irrigation systems.

1514 The population reaches 5,000. Funchal cathedral completed.

1566 Funchal sacked by French pirates; 300 islanders killed.
1580 Felipe II of Spain occupies Portugal; Madeira falls under Spanish rule.
1640 The Portuguese regain their kingdom (and Madeira).
1703 Britain is granted valuable trade concessions with Portugal. Many Britons settle on Madeira and soon dominate the wine trade.
1801–14 Napoleon occupies Portugal; British troops stationed on Madeira.
1850 European intellectuals and aristocrats 'discover' Madeira.
1872–3 Phylloxera destroys most of Madeira's vines. Bananas replace wine as the island's main cash crop.
1914–18 Portugal fights with the Allies in World War I.
1933 Salazar founds the Estado Novo and becomes dictator of Portugal.
1939–45 Portugal remains neutral in World War II.
1960 Madeira's first airport on Porto Santo opens.
1974 Bloodless revolution overthrows the dictatorship in Portugal.
1976 Madeira becomes an autonomous region with its own parliament.
1986 Portugal joins the EEC; gets funds to improve infrastructure.
1989 The first stretch of the Via Rápida motorway opens.
2010 Flash floods cause a mud slide that kills 40 people.
2012 With EU funds drying up and Madeira's debts estimated at €6 billion, President Alberto João Jardim courts private investors.
2015 Miguel Albuquerque becomes the new president of Madeira.
2016 Wildfires ravage the island, destroying 150 homes.
2020 The Covid-19 pandemic hits Madeira, disrupting the local economy for two years.
2023 Madeira is awarded EarthCheck Silver status as a Sustainable Tourism Destination.
2024 Wildfires burn more than 5,700 hectares of forest.
2025 Big-wave surfers ride what's considered Madeira's biggest swell of the decade, at the Jardim do Mar point break.

The mighty headland of Cabo Girão, on the western coast

Places

Getting around

Madeira's size can be deceptive. At first glance it might seem that two days would be sufficient to see the whole 57 by 22km (35 by 13 miles). Indeed, it is possible to speed from Funchal to once-remote Porto Moniz in under an hour. But to do so means travelling mainly in tunnels. For a taste of the island's beautiful scenery, there is no alternative but to take to Madeira's mountainous terrain and winding, two-lane roads.

A minimum of three days is necessary to see a good portion of the island; a full week allows you to do it justice and take the time to enjoy its scenic outdoors at a relaxed pace. The easiest option is to hop aboard day-trip buses that take in the main attractions: although the roads have improved, travelling by car is best undertaken by confident drivers who are comfortable negotiating steep, winding terrain.

More and more visitors are choosing to stay outside Funchal, and some of these barely set foot in the capital; accommodation in mountain lodges, country cottages and smaller coastal hotels has greatly improved over the years, appealing to those looking for an outdoorsy holiday or a wellness-focused break.

Funchal

Highlights

- **The city centre**, see page 35
- **The market and Old Town**, see page 43
- **West of town**, see page 46
- **Glorious gardens**, see page 47

Funchal ❶, capital of the Madeira Islands, is the only town of any size on Madeira – indeed in the entire archipelago – and most of

Madeira's historic buildings, museums and sights are located here. You could easily spend your entire trip in the city, and many visitors do. The best way to enjoy Funchal, however, is to regard it as a gateway to the sea and to the rest of the island, combining time in town with boat trips and excursions to the botanical gardens on the outskirts, or up into the mountains and along the wild southwest, north and eastern coasts. Even if you plan to spend most of your trip hiking, boating or canyoning, the city makes a useful base, since it's the hub for the island's bus networks and outdoor activity companies.

With a population of around 106,000, Funchal is a larger city than most expect to find on such a small island, but you can walk across the centre in just 15 minutes or so. Exploring inland to the north on foot is more difficult, as the streets become very steep. Nevertheless, walking remains the most practical way to see Funchal. The narrow, cobbled streets were never meant for vehicles, and those that are not pedestrianised can get surprisingly congested with traffic.

One way to get your bearings upon arrival is to walk out on the jetty known as the **Ilhéu de Pontinha** and view the city as those aboard cruise ships do. It's an outstanding panorama: white houses with terracotta roofs climb steeply through tropical greenery all around the spacious bay, with rugged mountains forming an attractive backdrop. The Pontinha, which was built in 1962, leads round the fishing harbour and ferry terminal, passing an old fortress that houses the **Design Centre Nini Andrade Silva** (www.niniandradesilva.com; free), an exhibition centre and restaurant created by Funchal-born Andrade Silva, one of Portugal's leading avant-garde interior designers, perched on top of what was once a tiny island known as Looe Rock.

Funchal's deep natural harbour propelled the city's development in the fifteenth and sixteenth centuries, when Madeira became known to those making expeditions to the Far East and the Americas. The busy port hosts cruise ships, yachts and picturesque (and functioning) fishing boats. The commercial freight port of Caniçal is about 28km (17 miles) northeast of Funchal.

The city centre

Funchal is every inch a maritime city, with a busy harbour and 210-berth marina. The **city centre** comprises a spacious seafront backed by a modest grid of elegant streets and squares arranged around the archipelago's only cathedral, which dates back to the fifteenth century. The dominant building on Avenida do Mar, the seafront road, is the fortress-like **Palácio de São Lourenço** (St Lawrence Palace; http://representantedarepublica-madeira.pt; free). Erected in the sixteenth century, it guarded the bay against pirates – you can see the ancient cannons poking through the crenellated walls. In the grand interior, there's a gallery of royal portraits.

Funchal and its harbour

Avenida do Mar has a palm-fringed promenade, partly adorned with beautiful black-on-white geometric cobbles, and a waterfront park, **Praça do Povo** (People's Square), dotted with pop-up cafés, bars, snack bars and selfie spots. Always lively, the square really comes alive during Funchal's many festivals and public events, with enthusiastic crowds milling around its performance spaces and food trucks. The Monumento ao Emigrante Madeirense, a 1980s bronze statue of a man on one knee, holding a globe aloft, represents Madeira's emigrants and is a focus for the island's Portugal Day ceremony in June. Other monuments in the square include a serene bust of Mahatma Gandhi, installed in 2019 to commemorate the 150th anniversary of the great peace-maker's birth, and a colourful tribute to Nelson Mandela in the shape of his intials.

Opposite the park is the **Assembleia Legislativa da Região Autónoma da Madeira** (Legislative Assembly), built in the 1980s as an extension to the **Alfândega Velha** (Old Customs House), while immediately to the west is the **Porto de Recreio** (marina), a starting point for dolphin and whale watching boat trips.

At the junction of Avenida Zarco and the main street, Avenida Arriaga, stands Francisco Franco's 1927 statue of João Gonçalves Zarco, the Portuguese navigator who discovered Madeira in the 1410s. Franco's work can be seen all over the city and at the **Museu Henrique e Francisco Franco** (Rua João de Deus 13; https://cultura.madeira.gov.pt; free). The imposing **Palácio do Governo Regional** Ⓐ, a handsome building with tiled patios and the administrative headquarters of Madeira, rises behind the Zarco monument to the right.

WHERE TO SHOOT THE BEST PICTURES

Ponta de São Lourenço. Perfect in the early morning light.
Pico Areeiro. Miradouro do Juncal and Miradouro do Ninho da Manta, close to the start of the Vereda do Areeiro hiking trail, are magical at sunrise (though hugely popular, so often crowded).
Seixal beach. With dark sand backed by jungle-clad cliffs, this north coast beach has an exotic, dramatic look.
Fanal forest. Fanal's ancient, twisted trees create a uniquely mysterious atmosphere, particularly on misty days.
Levada Fajã do Rodrigues. One of Madeira's most picturesque levada trails, with waterfalls, ferns, moss and lush laurisilva forest.

Avenida Arriaga is particularly pretty in late spring, when the jacaranda trees are in full bloom. At no.16, you will find the **tourist information office** and, next door, the **Adegas de São Francisco** (Blandy's Wine Lodge, Avenida Arriaga 28; www.blandyswinelodge.com; charge), Madeira's oldest working wine lodge. This atmospheric place was part of a Franciscan monastery, built in the seventeenth century. On a tour of this temple to the island's eponymous tipple, you'll learn about the wine-making process and visit the warm attics where fragrant wines mature in huge oak barrels, a process called *canteiro*. Even if you don't take a tour, you can visit the handsome tasting room, decorated with frescoes painted by the German artist Max Römer, in 1922.

Palácio de São Lourenço

Just a few steps west of the lodge is the small **Jardim Municipal de São Francisco** (St Francis' Garden), a delightful urban oasis with lush tropical vegetation. Across from the park is the **Teatro Municipal** (https://teatrobaltazardias.funchal.pt), a miniature gem from the 1880s that hosts periodic concerts, plays and films, and **The Ritz** (www.theritzmadeira.com), an elegant café with regular live music. It was once the Chamber of Commerce and has fine *azulejo* (blue and white tile) vignettes that depict scenes from old Madeira.

Towards the centre, at the east end of Avenida Arriaga, is Funchal's principal landmark, the **Sé** **B** (Cathedral, Rua do Aljube;

Funchal's Sé (Cathedral) is one of the island's oldest buildings

www.catedraldofunchal.com; free). Begun in 1493 and completed in 1517, the cathedral is one of the few buildings in Funchal to survive from the early days of colonisation. On completion, it was the headquarters of the largest diocese in the world, covering the entire Portuguese empire. The exterior is plain and simple, with stone-and-whitewash walls topped by a granite clock tower, but the cathedral's interior is is far more lavish, as you'd expect of a cathedral funded by King Manuel I of Portugal and a coterie of wealthy sugar merchants. To admire some of its most spectacular flourishes, look up: it has a splendid timber ceiling, inlaid with ivory and adorned in the *alfarje* (Mudéjar knotwork) style, inspired by Moorish geometrical patterns. The beautifully carved choir stalls in the sanctuary depict saints and prophets dressed like medieval merchants, and the huge Gothic altarpiece, a gilded polyptych, was shipped all the way from Lisbon.

Near the cathedral, on Praça de Colombo, the **Museu a Cidade do Açúcar** (City of Sugar Museum; https://cultura.madeira.gov.pt; free) tells the story of the island's fifteenth-century sugar trade through sculptures, paintings and artefacts. In the early days of the colony, Madeira's slopes bristled with sugar cane plantations and sugar production drove the economy.

Walking up Rua João Tavira, north of the cathedral, note the beautiful black and white mosaics beneath your feet, typical of historic Portuguese towns, and explore the pretty narrow shopping streets to the right. At the top of Rua João Tavira is **Praça do Município** ❸, the town's dignified main square, with a fish-scale mosaic pavement and historic buildings on all sides. On the northern side is the seventeenth-century **Igreja de São João Evangelista do Colégio** (Collegiate Church; free), originally founded by the Jesuits in 1629. A spacious and airy old place, it is decorated with seventeenth- and eighteenth-century tiles, paintings and gilt woodcarving.

At the head of the square (to the northeast) stands the **Câmara Municipal** (Town Hall; http://cmf.aauma.pt; charge), which occupies a a palace built in 1758 for a local aristocrat, the Conde de Carvahal. Don't miss the graceful, nineteenth-century statue of *Leda e o Cisne (Leda and the Swan)* in the inner courtyard. The statue used to be in the old fish market – a fact that is corroborated by the tiled panel outside the present municipal market. There's another famous statue in the town hall's small garden on Rua do Padre Gonçalves da Câmara: *O Semeador* (The Sower), a modernist bronze by celebrated Madeiran sculptor Francisco Franco (see page 43).

NOTES

The building that houses the University of Madeira, to the north of the Praça do Município, was formerly a Jesuit College that also served as a barracks for British troops during the nineteenth century.

On the square's south side is the **Museu de Arte Sacra** D (Museum of Religious Art; www.masf.pt; charge), Madeira's most important art museum. It is housed in a seventeenth-century palace, the former residence of the bishop of Funchal. The outstanding works on view include a dozen or so fifteenth- and sixteenth-century Flemish paintings, regarded as among the richest in Portugal and rare even in the rest of Europe. These vibrant masterpieces, as well as other excellent works from the Portuguese school of the same period, were donated to the island's churches by Madeira's wealthy sugar merchants, who during the sixteenth century traded their 'white gold' in Antwerp, which was then the home of a thriving artistic culture. There is also a fine collection of Flemish sculpture, as well as goldsmithery.

Volcanic stone is used to make mosaic pavements

The main door of the museum leads to Rua do Bispo (Bishop Street) and both this and the parallel street, Rua Queimada Cima, are well worth exploring for their shops, cafés and historic buildings.

Continue west from the Praça do Municipio on Rua da Carreira, a bustling street full of popular old-fashioned shops and affordable restaurants. On the left is the **Museu de Fotografia da Madeira (Atelier Vicente's)** (Rua da Carreira 43; https://cultura.madeira.gov.pt;

charge) with photographs reflecting 150 years of island life. They're the work of Funchal's leading photo studio, founded by Vicente Gomes da Silva in 1846. He and his sons had numerous high-profile subjects, including Empress Elizabeth of Austria, the Empress of Brazil and Winston Churchill, on his 1950 visit to Câmara de Lobos.

Stone Manueline window, Quinta das Cruzes

Further down the Rua da Carreira is the picturesque Rua da Mouraria, with antiques shops and the **Museu de História Natural** (Rua da Mouraria 31; https://cultura.madeira.gov.pt; charge), another eighteenth-century aristocratic home converted into a museum. Its simply presented cabinets of taxidermy focus on the birds, mammals, fish and insects of Madeira, plus rocks and minerals. Old-fashioned but packed with interest, the exhibits include some fearsome marine species: sharks, ocean sunfish and the like.

At the top of the street is the charming **Igreja de São Pedro** (Rua de São Pedro 1; free), built in the sixteenth century. Its walls are lined entirely with blue and white *azulejo* tiles and it has a beautifully painted wood ceiling, fine chandeliers, a massive gilded altar and valuable paintings.

About halfway up the steep Calçada de Santa Clara, at No. 7, you reach the **Casa Museu Frederico de Freitas** (De Freitas

Stalls at the Mercado dos Lavradores

House and Museum; https://cultura.madeira.gov.pt; charge). It is divided into two parts: the modern wing is dedicated to *azulejos* and their history, along with other decorative tiles from sources such as Turkey, Syria and Holland. The old mansion alongside, the Casa de Calçada, is full of paintings of Madeira from the seventeenth to nineteenth centuries, and the furnishings of an affluent nineteenth-century household.

Continue uphill to the **Convento de Santa Clara** (https://cultura.madeira.gov.pt; charge). Built towards the end of the fifteenth century and expanded two centuries later, it is one of Madeira's most outstanding heritage sites. The church is a splendid building, with walls completely covered by rare seventeenth-century *azulejos* in geometric patterns, and with a fine painted ceiling. The ornate tomb at the back of the church is sometimes mistaken for that of Zarco, the island's discoverer; in fact, it is the tomb of his son-in-law – Zarco's humbler grave lies beneath the modern timber floor of the high altar.

During his stint as governor of the island, Zarco lived a short way up Calçada do Pico, in the **Quinta das Cruzes** Ⓔ (https://mqc.madeira.gov.pt/en; charge). Constructed in the fifteenth century, but rebuilt after an earthquake in 1748 and expanded in the nineteenth century, this is Funchal's finest *quinta* (villa) open to the public. The main house is a museum of antiques: superb sixteenth-century Indo-Portuguese and seventeenth-century Madeiran as well as eighteenth- and nineteenth-century English pieces. The house is surrounded by a lovely, somewhat unkempt garden of exotic flowers, trees and plants.

Rua das Cruzes, the road separating Quinta das Cruzes from the convent, leads to a lookout point with a view over the town, the port and the dome of the English Church.

The market and Old Town

Between two *ribeiras* (river beds) that carry excess water from the mountains to the sea, is Rua Dr Fernão Ornelas, lined with old shops, it leads to Funchal's central market. In spring, the little rivers are hidden beneath trellises of blazing bougainvillea. Directly ahead lies the **Mercado dos Lavradores** Ⓕ (Workers' Market, Rua Brigadeiro Oudinout; http://mercados.funchal.pt), housed in a two-storey, open-roofed hall adorned with large tiled panels painted with scenes from Madeira's rural regions. It's open daily except Sunday, but the best time to visit is on Friday or Saturday, when fishermen, farmers and traders from all over the island pour into town. The market is bustling, fragrant and colourful, with flower sellers dressed in traditional costume (red and yellow striped skirts, red waistcoats and black caps), and stalls laden with fruit and vegetables of all shapes, colours and sizes including lomquats, tomarillos and pitangas, grown on the island. Meat and fish stalls can be found in separate areas: worth noting is the gloriously ugly *espada* (scabbard fish) that frequently features on Madeiran menus and is something of a rarity as it is only caught here and off the coast of Japan. There are also several wicker and handicraft shops.

The market marks the start of the **Zona Velha** ⓖ (Old Town). The main streets are the narrow, cobbled alleyway of Rua de Santa Maria and, parallel, Rua Dom Carlos I. This once run-down fishermen's quarter has been transformed into a lively, bohemian area of poncha bars, restaurants and galleries, with street art, a seafront promenade and a cable-car taking passengers up to the famous hill village of Monte (see page 49).

The view from the Fortaleza de São Tiago

Near the cable car station is a popular attraction called the **Madeira Story Centre** (Rua Dom Carlos I 27; www.madeirastorycentre.com; charge), packed with exhibits, videos and interactive displays recounting the history of the archipelago, from its volcanic origins to the modern era. Its galleries delve into topics such as the age of discovery, the development of the Madeira wine trade and the early days of tourism.

NOTES

The creators of the striking Casino Park Hotel were the Brazilian architect Oscar Niemeyer and the Portuguese architect Alfredo Viana de Lima. Aware that its proportions and style would raise eyebrows, Niemeyer urged the local authorities to implement planning restrictions that would protect Madeira's picturesque landscapes. Niemeyer also designed the adjoining casino, which is built in the shape of a giant crown of thorns.

One of the busiest parts of the Zona Velha is the row of restaurants at the pedestrian-only eastern end, beyond which lies the **Capela do Corpo Santo** (Chapel of the Body of Christ, Largo do Corpo Santo; free). The chapel, dating from the end of the fifteenth century, is one of the oldest in Funchal, built by a charity supporting the local fishermen. Its gabled facade and the remaining Gothic doorway are original features. The low houses beyond once housed fishing families, but are gradually being taken over by artisans making leather sandals or selling lace and embroidery.

At the far end of the Old Town is the **Fortaleza de São Tiago** (Fort of St James). Built in the seventeenth century and expanded in the middle of the eighteenth, this picturesque fort served as a barracks for British troops during the Napoleonic Wars. The site has been used for various purposes, including headquarters for the British forces and Army Police. It now houses a good restaurant with views along the cliffs that rise to the east of Funchal.

Formal gardens at the Jardim Botânico

West of town

Avenida Arriaga ends at the Rotunda do Infante, where a statue of Prince Henry the Navigator sits at the easternmost tip of **Parque de Santa Catarina** ⓗ (St Catherine's Park; free). A delightful hilltop retreat, this is Funchal's largest park, with splendid views over the marina. Aside from the gardens, lake and playground, other points of interest include the Capela de Santa Catarina from 1425, said to be the island's oldest chapel. At the west end of the park, the elegant pink **Quinta Vigia** is the official residence of the president of Madeira.

Above the park looms the uncompromisingly massive Casino Park Hotel. When it opened in 1976, it was the largest hotel in Portugal, with 379 rooms and an improbably airy-looking lattice of concrete balconies, seemingly levitating over a sweeping lawn. The Casino Park signals the start of the traditional hotel zone, flush with five-star hotels such as the Savoy Palace, Cliff Bay, Royal Savoy, the Pestana Carlton and Reid's Palace, plus a few *quintas* and posh restaurants.

On the waterfront, the **Museu CR7** (Avenida Sá Carneiro 27; www.museucr7.com; charge) dedicated to Cristiano Ronaldo, who was born on the island, is a must for all football fans: it displays dozens of his trophies, jerseys, shoes and other memorabilia, has screens showing big moments from his career, including classic goals. You can even have your picture taken with Ronaldo's 3D augmented reality avatar. North of Reid's Palace stands **MAMMA** (Museu de Arte Moderna na Madeira; www.mamma-museum.pt; charge), a private gallery that sometimes hosts live concerts. To the west the *Zona Hoteleira* stretches along the clifftops, lined with resort complexes and a seafront promenade featuring cafés and swimming pools, including the **Complexo Balnear do Lido** (Rua do Gorgulho 11; www.frentemarfunchal.pt; charge), a spacious and hugely popular collection of saltwater swimming pools and sun terraces.

Glorious gardens

A short bus or taxi ride into the hillsides northeast of Funchal (on the road to Camacha) takes you to the wonderful **Jardim Botânico da Madeira** ❶ (Botanical Garden of Madeira; https://ifcn.madeira.gov.pt; charge), the most comprehensive public garden on the

CLIFFTOP PALACE

Standing high over Funchal harbour is Reid's, one of the world's most famous hotels. It was begun by William Reid, a Scot who arrived on Madeira aged 14 in 1836, having run away to sea. He became a prosperous wine merchant in Funchal and by the age of 25 was also renting and managing *quintas* for well-to-do invalids from northern Europe. He converted some of the villas into hotels, and in due course acquired the clifftop site for the luxury hotel of his dreams. He died before it could be finished, and the project was completed by his sons Willy and Albert. Reid's finally opened its doors in 1891. In 1937, the hotel passed into the hands of the Blandy family, another famous British-Madeiran dynasty, and in 1996, it was acquired by the Orient-Express group, which has refurbished it without sacrificing any of its fin de siècle grandeur, and restored its original name, Reid's Palace (although now prefixed by Belmond). It remains the epitome of upper-class luxury, and eminent guests over the years have included Sir Winston Churchill, Charles I of Austria, General Batista of Cuba, and the writer George Bernard Shaw, who signed up for dancing lessons here at the grand age of 71.

island. A wonderland for any plant-lover, the gardens have examples of virtually every plant that grows on Madeira and lots of subtropical flowers and plants from far-flung destinations. It occupies steep terraces that offer fine views over Funchal.

The **Teleférico do Jardim Botânico** (Botanical Garden Cable Car; www.telefericojardimbotanico.com; charge) offers the chance to glide high above the green ravine northwest of the Botanical Garden and up to the hill town of Monte (see page 49). It is a fantastic trip.

The **Jardins da Quinta da Boa Vista** (Rua Luís Figueiroa de Albuquerque; charge) on the eastern side of the city is a busy working farm dedicated to orchids. Set in the grounds of a beautiful 200-year-old villa, it was founded in the 1960s and has

The luxuriant Palheiro Gardens

received numerous awards, most notably from the British Royal Horticultural Society.

But the most splendid of Madeira's horticultural wonders are the **Palheiro Gardens** ❶ www.palheironatureestate.com; charge). The hillside estate, only a short bus ride from Funchal to the east of the city, is the property of the family that once owned Reid's Hotel (see page 47) and is one of the famous producers of Madeira wine. Built in the 1820s, the *quinta* has been in the hands of the Blandy family for more than a century. The gardens are famous for their winter-flowering camellias. The long, cobbled entrance avenue is shaded by plane trees, while the fields that lie on either side are carpeted with a wonderful spread of arum and belladonna lilies in spring, and agapanthus in summer and autumn. Formal and informal areas are landscaped with pools and fountains, while terraces tumble down the hillsides.

Around Funchal

Highlights

- **Monte**, see below
- **Villages in the hills**, see page 53

A number of excellent visits are within easy reach of Funchal, so be sure to make the most of its surroundings. Tour operators often promote Monte, Camacha and Curral das Freiras as popular half-day excursions.

Monte

The hilltop village of **Monte** ❷, 550m (1,804 feet) above sea level, has been fashionable ever since wealthy nineteenth century merchants built their splendid *quintas* up here in the cool air above Funchal. Later, in 1921, the exiled Karl I (Charles I of Austria, the last of the Austro-Hungarian emperors) and his wife Zita fleetingly

DOWNHILL RACERS

Monte's famous and hugely popular wicker street toboggans were used at the beginning of the nineteenth century to carry freight down the frighteningly steep 5km (3-mile) hill between Monte and Funchal. A British merchant, living in Monte and weary of winding his way down to Funchal every day, hit on the idea that the same toboggans could carry people. A wicker seat was fixed to the basic sled and so the *carros de cesto* (literally basket-cars) were born. Each *carro* is controlled by two *carreiros*, wearing traditional straw boaters, who give an initial push and then ride along until another push, or pull, or sudden brake, is required, depending on the desired speed and any traffic ahead. For brakes they use the rubber soles of their boots.

The modern toboggan ride (www.carreirosdomonte.com; charge) is purely a tourist attraction, and a pale shadow of its former self, but fun nonetheless. Even though the fares are worthy of a high-tech roller-coaster, it's a relatively sedate experience, since the road surface is no longer the low-friction cobbles that had *carros* careering down the hill. The lot of the *carreiros* has also improved. They used to have to walk back up the hill, carrying or pushing the 68kg (150lb) sleds, but nowadays they make the journey by truck.

made the village their home. Today, it is perhaps best known for the toboggan rides that originate here, and the cable cars that link Monte with Funchal's Old Town (Teleférico do Funchal; www.madeiracablecar.com; charge) and the Jardim Botânico (Teleférico Jardim Botânico; www.telefericojardimbotanico.com; charge). Gliding up to Monte by cable car is a classic Funchal experience. The cabins carry up to seven passengers, the ride takes 15–20 minutes and there are glorious views of the bay, the capital and leafy suburbs on the way. On arrival, the main reasons to linger in Monte are to pause over a coffee, visit its church and wander through its gardens (see page 47).

Monte's main square is on the western side of the village, and is a pleasant evocation of yesteryear. The rack-and-pinion railway that once laboured up the ferociously steep hill closed in the 1930s, but the railway station is still here on the western side of the tree-shaded square, and the viaduct arches now rise over the perfectly clipped public gardens of the **Parque Municipal do Monte**, established in 1894 (https://cultura.madeira.gov.pt; free).

A short walk up a path from the square is the elegant and richly decorated **Igreja de Nossa Senhora do Monte** (Our Lady of Monte; www.pnsmonte.pt; free). Dedicated to Madeira's patron saint, it is even more important to the islanders than Funchal's Sé: to the many Madeirans who believe that the Virgin Mary has

Transport by wicker toboggan

Curral das Freiras, the Refuge of the Nuns

carried them through troubled times, it's akin to Lourdes. On the Feast of the Assumption, 15 August, thousands make a pilgrimage to the church. This is also a time of revels, which kick off on the evening of 14 August. Others come throughout the year to pray at the chapel on the left of the church that holds the tomb of Karl I of Austria, who died on Madeira in 1922, and whose path to sainthood was prepared when he was beatified by Pope John Paul II in 2004 for his efforts to end World War I. At the foot of the church steps is the starting point of the **Carros de Cesto** – the downhill ride aboard a wicker street toboggan (see page 50).

The **Jardim Tropical Monte Palace** (Monte Palace Tropical Gardens; www.montepalacemadeira.com; charge), a short walk east of the church, is firmly rooted in the past. The gardens that surround the château-like Monte Palace – once the area's most fashionable hotel – are home to hundreds of plants and various other displays. The influential Madeiran South African entrepreneur José Manuel Rodrigues Berardo bought this seven hectare estate as a passion project in the 1980s, and set about restoring and beautifying it. The gardens are lushly beautiful, with an impressive collection of native and exotic flora (especially good cycads), a koi pond, a porcelain collection and historical artefacts from throughout Portugal, including architectural pieces taken from important buildings and prized *azulejo* panels. The views of Funchal are unbeatable. The **Museu Monte Palace** within the gardens houses more than 1,000 sculptures and a unique collection of precious and semi-precious stones from around the world.

The commanding hillside viewpoint of **Terreiro da Luta**, a stiff 1.8km walk or winding 3km drive above Monte, offers another magnificent panorama of Funchal. It was here that the figure of Our Lady of Monte (now in the church below) was allegedly discovered in the fifteenth century. On the summit is a monument to Nossa Senhora da Paz (Our Lady of Peace), dedicated to the end of World War I. Around the monument are anchor chains from French ships sunk in Funchal harbour by German torpedoes.

Villages in the hills

A good half-day excursion by bus, taxi or organised tour is the 16km (10-mile) trip north on the narrow, twisting road to Curral das Freiras 3 (Refuge of the Nuns), a village surrounded by extinct volcanoes that has been isolated from the outside world for much of its history. The nuns in question fled here from Funchal's Santa Clara Convent in the sixteenth century to escape raiding pirates. Protected on all sides by mountains and supported by rich volcanic soil and abundant sunshine, their settlement became permanent. The village continued in splendid isolation until the late 1950s, when the first road tunnels were bored through the mountains. Television finally reached the village in 1986, and the 2.5km VE6 tunnel was completed in 2004.

Curral das Freiras is famous for its cherries and chestnuts: it's the main source for the roasted chestnuts that Funchal's street vendors sell in the autumn, and there's a lively harvest festival, the Festa da Castanha, in late October or early November. The village shops sell locally made *ginja* (cherry liqueur) and *licor de castanha* (chestnut liqueur) all year round.

The best way to appreciate the scale of the valley is from above. The view from the lookout point of **Eira do Serrado** (1,006 metres/ 3,300ft) is breathtaking. An alternative view is from the southwest, across the valley, at the lookout point **Boca dos Namorados** (Lovers' Nest), a stop often included in 4WD tours. From here, the panorama sweeps round and takes in the entire valley (though even at 1,100 metres/3,608ft you will still be close enough to hear the bell of the village church).

The lighthouse at Ponta do Pargo, the island's western tip

Around 16km (10 miles) northeast of Funchal is **Camacha**, a pretty village at nearly 700 metres (2,300ft). In the heart of willow country, it is the island's centre of the wickerwork industry. Many of the local inhabitants are employed crafting furniture, table mats, baskets and other household items. Around Camacha, and especially to the north of here, you are likely to see the stripped willow soaked and left to dry, either by a riverbank, propped up against a house, or in wigwam fashion in the fields. The village is also also known for its lively folk music and dance tradition and for its Apple Festival, held in October.

Camacha is the starting point for two excellent *levada* walks heading west to Vale do Paraíso and northeast to Eira de Fora. To enjoy these walks without getting lost, you need a guide or a walking guidebook, such as Sunflower Books' ultra-reliable *Walk & Eat Madeira* (see page 136).

Western Madeira

Highlights

- **Câmara de Lobos and Cabo Girão**, see below
- **Ribeira Brava**, see page 57
- **The southwest coast**, see page 57
- **The northwest coast**, see page 60

Western Madeira begins just beyond the capital's hotel zone. Here, the pace is slower and the coast even less discovered than further east. It was only a matter of time before tourism would creep in this direction, but the lofty cliffs, mountainsides and ravines don't lend themselves to large resort hotels; instead, most of the places to stay are appealing, eco-chic boutique hotels and agroturismo cottages. Inland offers some gloriously wild countryside, excellent for hiking and canyoning, while in the north, there are pretty villages with inviting natural pools, carved out of lava.

Câmara de Lobos and Cabo Girão

Just 8.5km (5.3 miles) west of Funchal is **Câmara de Lobos** ❹ (Lair of the Seals). It's close enough to Funchal to feel like a satellite of the capital, but with its steadfast fishing, dining and drinking culture, it has a salty character that's very much its own. Its name refers to the Mediterranean monk seals that once swam near here.

In 1950, Winston Churchill spent time on the island painting the fishing port, an interest that ensured its standing as an idyllic, old-world fishing village. The gaily painted boats are still here, as is the protected, natural rocky harbour.

Gentrification and a lively smattering of restaurants have crept in to the once-impoverished port area, but there's still plenty of macho swagger to the harbourside bars, where hard-drinking locals play cards and down *poncha* (sugar-cane brandy, lemon juice and honey) while grizzled old fishermen repair their boats on the shore. Close to the waterfront is the Fishermen's Chapel, where locals give thanks for the villagers' safe return from the sea. The regenerated islet of Câmara de Lobos, a cliff (resembling an island)

Picturesque Câmara de Lobos is still an active fishing village

where the fishermen used to live, is now a public garden with stunning sea views.

West of Câmara de Lobos, the coastal road climbs through rich agricultural country, famous for grapes and bananas. It peaks at the top of the mighty headland known as **Cabo Girão** ❺. One of the highest sea cliffs in the world, it plummets 590 metres (1,900ft) to the Atlantic. The views east and west along the coast are sensational. There's a terrifying, exhilarating viewpoint (Miradouro do Cabo Girão; https://simplifica.madeira.gov.pt; charge), where you stand on a glass floor, clutching a glass-panelled rail, with nothing else beneath you save the sweep of the wild sea hundreds of metres below. Hundreds of metres below, farmers have managed to salvage tiny plots of arable land, terracing them on the sides and base of the cliff.

Ribeira Brava

The next major settlement, heading west, is **Ribeira Brava** ❻. If you are in a hurry, it can be reached in just 20 minutes on the *Via Rápida* from Funchal. This orderly little community, founded in 1440, lies at the southern end of a mighty and superbly scenic ravine that carves the island in two, from north to south. Except in winter, Ribeira Brava's river is more of a tame trickle.

The main focus is the sixteenth-century **Igreja de São Bento** (St Benedict's Church), with some of the island's finest gilded and carved woodwork, a nativity and an elaborate font. In Rua de São Francisco, the **Museu Etnográfico da Madeira** (Madeira Ethnographic Museum; https://cultura.madeira.gov.pt; charge) describes the fishing, farming and wine-making traditions that still just about survive in Madeira's more remote outposts.

The southwest coast

From Ribeira Brava, most coach excursions head north to São Vicente (see page 61), as the road cuts through some of the best scenery on the whole island. However, those with more time can continue along the southwest coast.

Ponta do Sol is the next village after Ribeira Brava. As its name suggests, it is blessed with more than its fair share of sunshine. Only during the summer does it really come alive, however, when beach umbrellas are set out above the stony beach. There are two buildings of note here. The eighteenth-century church, **Igreja de Nossa Senhora da Luz** (Church of Our Lady of Light), has a splendid painted ceiling, seventeenth century *azulejo* tiles and an interesting Mudejar style font, thought to have come from Seville. Ponta do Sol's arts centre, the **Centro Cultural John dos Passos**, (https://cultura.madeira.gov.pt; free) is housed in the restored

Bananas are big business along the south coast of Madeira

home of the American novelist's grandparents, who emigrated from this village in the mid-nineteenth century. The centre hosts temporary exhibitions, seminars, conferences and Ponta do Sol's **Digital Nomad Village** (www.digitalnomads.startupmadeira.eu), a free co-working space, funded by the Madeiran government. On the coast a little under 2km east of Ponta do Sol is the **BAM Centro da Banana da Madeira** (https://bam-centrodabananadamadeira.pt; charge) a cheerful and engaging agricultural innovation centre and attraction dedicated to Madeira's most abundant fruit.

There are yet more banana plantations surrounding **Calheta** ❼, the only town of significance as you continue west. It's southwest Madeira's principal beach resort, with a large artificial-sand beach, a marina bobbing with yachts, and Madeira's contemporary art museum, the **MUDAS Museu de Arte Contemporânea** (https://cultura.madeira.gov.pt; charge), located on the clifftop to the west of the town. Besides a collection of more than 400 works by Portuguese artists, MUDAS also houses an auditorium, a library, shop, café and restaurant. The Igreja Matriz do Espírito Santo, Calheta's parish church, features a handsome Moorish-style ceiling. Next door is the Sociedade dos Engenhos da Calheta, a sugar mill, which produces honey and rum. Thanks partly to the presence of MUDAS, Calheta feels more sophisticated than villagey Ponta do Sol, and attracts arty, food-loving types.

From Calheta, a steep inland road climbs to the very centre of the island, up to the **Paúl da Serra** ❽ (High Moorland). This remote plateau measures some 17 by 6km (11 by 3.5 miles), and presents a dramatic contrast to the rugged mountains elsewhere on Madeira. It can be foggy and bleak at times, but on clear days, it has commanding views across the island. If you are thinking of hiking here, be warned that mists descend suddenly; you may want to go with a guide (see page 132).

Where the road from Calheta joins the main road across the moorland, turn right for the large car park that serves **Rabaçal** ❾, a beautiful valley popular among Madeirans at weekends and holidays. Dense with mossy laurisilva forest, this region is uninhabited, and feels wild and remote. This is the starting point for a couple of spectacular *levada* walks (PR6.1 Levada do Risco and PR6 Levada das 25 Fontes; https://simplifica.madeira.gov.pt; charge). Both involve walking downhill from the car park along the narrow and twisting tarmac road that leads to the rest house and barbecue pits at Rabaçal, then following the signs. The 6km trip to the **Risco waterfall** and back is flat and takes about two hours. The 8.6-km hike to **25 Fontes** (25 Springs) – as the name suggests, a verdant and water-filled spot – takes around three hours and involves a pretty steep climb along the way. Both routes are wonderfully scenic.

The northwest coast

At the island's extreme northwestern tip, **Porto Moniz** ⑩, is well under 40km from Funchal as the crow flies, but seems a world away. Here, a tongue of volcanic lava that flowed into the Atlantic thousands of years ago has been carved by the waves into pools. Above, small plots of farmland climb the hills, sheltered from the salty wind by basalt walls and tree heather fencing. You could spend a happy hour or two on the shore, swimming, paddling in rock pools or simply sitting on the rocks and watching the sea. There are two areas of saltwater swimming pools on the coast in Porto Moniz, a few hundred metres apart. The main area is semi-natural,with steps and lifeguards (charge), while the other area is natural (free), with a wilder feel. Sculptural lava formations and clear water make them delightful places to swim.

Seixal ⑪ ('say-shall'), between Porto Moniz and São Vicente, lies in a vine-growing area. The Sercial grape, used to produce the driest style of Madeira wine, grows on impossible-seeming steep terraces behind this coastal village, protected from wind and salt-laden air by bracken fences. Tantalisingly, much of the VE2, the northwest coast road that connects Porto Moniz, Seixal and São Vicente, is swallowed by tunnels. Only a few sections have ocean views, so enjoy them each time you emerge. Inland from here is the atmospheric **Floresta do Fanal** (Fanal Forest), a peaceful place with ancient, twisted trees.

São Vicente ⓬, perhaps the prettiest village on the island, begins at the point where the northern coastal road meets the north–south road to Ribeira Brava. São Vicente's compact, well-kept centre is pedestrian-only, and attractive shops and cafés look onto Igreja Matriz, a lovely church, founded in the fifteenth century, with a painted ceiling depicting St Vincent. Set a little inland, the village is protected from the stiff sea breezes and usually feels

Natural swimming pools in the volcanic rock at Porto Moniz

very peaceful. With hills cloaked in native laurisilva forest, this is an appealing base for hikers.

Temporarily closed at the time of writing, the **Grutas e Centro do Vulcanismo** (www.grutasecentrodovulcanismosaovicente.com; charge), south of São Vicente, were created by gases blasting through molten lava from a now-extinct volcano in Paúl da Serra, that erupted around 890,000 years ago. The first scientist to explore them, in 1855, was James Yate Johnson, an English naturalist. There are no stalagmites and stalactites in these extraordinary tubes; atmospheric lighting highlights their lumpy contours.

High on a hill above the village is a distinctive tower standing over a small chapel dedicated to Our Lady of Fátima. This isolated

São Vicente, one of Madeira's most attractive villages

spot is a significant pilgrimage site, and its clock and chiming bells, icons of the region, can be seen and heard for miles around.

NOTES

Madeira is known for its microclimates. Even though it's a small island, the weather can change several times over the course of the day, or if you move just 5km (3 miles). Clouds come and go with great alacrity, so don't despair if a day starts overcast – the clouds may clear in a matter of minutes.

While the north-south ER104 highway tunnels through the mountains towards Ribeira Brava, the old road continues to cut its way upwards through verdant countryside until finally coming to a crest at the pass of **Boca da Encumeada** (626 metres/2,054ft). From here you can see right to the north coast and well into the south, while on each side are vast expanses of mountain scenery. This is one of the starting points for treks to Pico Ruivo (1,862 metres/6,109ft), Madeira's highest peak.

One of the best *levada* walks on the island (Route PR21 Caminho do Norte; https://simplifica.madeira.gov.pt; charge) skirts the edge of the mountain and takes in the entire valley, with views of the sea. Look for the steps opposite the Bar-Restaurant Boca da Encumeada. The walk along the irrigation canal is lined with hydrangeas and ferns. It's around a 45-minute walk until you reach a second tunnel. From here you can return to follow Levada das Rabaças for more amazing views.

The valley south of Boca da Encumeada, **Serra de Água**, contains the island's first hydroelectric power station (Madeira now has seven), amid a quiet agricultural community, tucked away in some of the island's lushest hills. Unfortunately for the forests and the locals, this region was hit hard by Madeira's 2024 wildfires. The road from here leads down into Ribeira Brava, where the *Via Rápida* motorway whisks you back to Funchal.

The central highlands

Highlights

- **Pico do Areeiro**, see below
- **Ribeiro Frio and the levada trails**, see page 66
- **The road to Santana**, see page 67

The rugged range of long-dormant volcanoes that splits the island into north and south makes weather forecasting difficult on Madeira. While it is usually warm and clear down in Funchal, the mountains are often shrouded in a wintry mist. But this doesn't necessarily mean that you will have no view once you start climbing. Mountain tops often jut through the clouds, a spectacular sight in itself. Madeira's microclimates are hard to judge, especially from below, so it's well worth scanning the island's webcams. If it looks clear first thing in the morning, follow the ER103 north from Funchal. By the time you get to the Poiso junction, you should know whether it's worth turning northwest to Pico do Arieeiro. Meanwhile, the ER103 continues north towards the coast, with beautiful vistas, secluded villages and exhilarating walks en route. The northern slopes of the mountains are cloaked in glorious, UNESCO World Heritage-listed laurisilva forest, rich in biodiversity and home to endemic species.

Pico do Areeiro

At 1,818 metres (5,900ft), **Pico do Areeiro** ⓭ (sometimes spelt Arieiro) is Madeira's third-highest mountain, and its summit is reachable by car. As the road rises, the rugged countryside becomes spectacularly barren, though plunging volcanic hillsides have been softened and greened by time.

The lookout point at the windswept, Mars-like summit provides a 360-degree panorama. With its stratified canyon walls, frozen lava and rust-red boulders, it's a geologist's dream. During summer, the terrain is parched, while at other times it is often covered with snow. The overnight temperature plunges below freezing most of the year, while the average annual temperature is below 10°C (50°F). There is also six times as much rain here as in Funchal. If the arrival of clouds catches you unaware, take refuge in the café on the summit.

At 1,861 metres (6,105ft), **Pico Ruivo**, the 'rooftop of Madeira', is only fractionally higher than Pico do Arieiro, but much less accessible. The peak can be reached by a walk of approximately one hour from Achada do Teixeira in the north, or the classic but strenuous four-hour round-trip hike from Pico do Arieiro (Routes PR1.2 Vereda do Pico Ruivo and PR1 Vereda do Areeiro; https://simplifica.madeira.gov.pt; charge). The latter is well signposted and there is a paved

Mountains near Pico de Arieiro

footpath, with drops protected by railings. The trek is a popular activity; on a good day you will see several other walkers here, so don't worry about losing your way. Warm clothing and hiking boots are essential, though, and in winter conditions can be hazardous, with icy winds, slippery mud and landslides damaging the path. If you suffer from vertigo it is best not to even attempt the walk.

Ribeiro Frio and the levada trails

Back on the main road, north of Poiso, is the enchanting **Ribeiro Frio** ⓮, more a bend in the road than a town. Tucked into a valley that, as its name (Cold Brook) suggests, can be sunless and rather chilly, this forested hamlet is the starting point for superb hikes

Hikers on Pico Ruivo

and canyoning trips. If it's raining, pop into Restaurante Ribeiro Frio, which resembles an Alpine chalet, warming visitors with log fires and freshly grilled trout from the hatchery across the road. Adjacent to the restaurant is a tiny chapel and a small botanical garden that claims to have examples of every native species of flower, plant and tree to be found on Madeira.

The shorter of the two walks that begin from Ribeiro Frio is an out-and-back route totalling 3km (Route PR11 Vereda do Balcões; https://simplifica.madeira.gov.pt; charge), visiting the outstanding Balconies lookout. After a stroll through the woods, you reach a series of platforms that seem suspended in mid-air, with stupendous views across steep hillsides and dramatic ravines to the distinctive peaks of Ruivo and Areeiro. If it's not hidden in cloud, the sight certainly ranks as one of the most beautiful on the island. The second walk (Route PR10 Levada do Furado; https://simplifica.madeira.gov.pt; charge) is one of the island's most popular *levada* trails (see page 132). This 11km walk takes around five hours to complete. Follow the signs for **Portela**, the end of the route; you may wish to arrange for a taxi to pick you up from here.

The road to Santana

North of Ribeiro Frio, towards the coast, is **Faial**, set picturesquely at the foot of the Penha d'Águia (Eagle Rock). There are fine views of its cliff face from the Miradouro do Guindaste, on the coast northeast of the village. Faial's swimming beach, a sheltered cove of dark pebbles called **Foz da Ribeira do Faial**, is reached via the rather circuitous Estrada da Praia do Faial.

Santana ⓯ is home to an unashamedly adorable style of building – A-framed cottages known as *palheiros*. The classic *palheiro* is a two-storey white stucco house with a brightly painted red door, red and blue window-frames and shutters and a thatched roof. Two particularly tidy *palheiros* have become tourist attractions because they're in the centre of the village (one houses a

Following a levada trail

tourist information centre). Cowsheds in a similar style dot the hillsides nearby.

There are more *palheiros* to explore in the grounds of the north **Parque Temático do Madeira** (Madeira Theme Park; www.parquetematicodamadeira.pt; charge). Set in three hectares (seven acres) of land, this is an enjoyable attraction for children, with rock-climbing walls, playgrounds and a boating lake, plus some good displays on the ecology, history, customs and landscape of the Madeiran islands.

Thatched houses of a larger, more conventional kind are to be found 5km (3 miles) south of Santana, in **Queimadas**, a complex of cottage-style rest houses with attractive gardens, set in the midst of a UNESCO-listed forest that's a lovely spot for a picnic.

If the weather is clear you might take the opportunity to ascend to the island's highest peak. This is reached by following the ER218 southwest out of Santana, through the Pico das Pedras forest, up to **Achada do Teixeira** at 1,592 metres (5,223ft). From here, it is a two-hour round-trip walk (Route PR1.2 Vereda do Pico Ruivo; https://simplifica.madeira.gov.pt; charge) to Pico Ruivo (see page 65).

The scenery northwest of Santana is just as delightful. **São Jorge** has a richly ornamented historic church, while past the village there is a splendid panorama from the *miradouro* at **Cabanas**, over to the valley of Arco de São Jorge.

The road winds inland towards the picturesque, fertile countryside around **Fajã do Penedo** and on to the pretty village of **Boaventura**. To cool off in a seafront lido, follow the coast road down to the small peninsula of **Ponta Delgada**, where the church next to the lido has a flamboyant ceiling painting depicting biblical stories. From here it's just 5km (3 miles) to São Vicente, at which point the road heads south to Ribeira Brava, then east back to Funchal.

Eastern Madeira

Highlights

- **Machico**, see page 70
- **The northeast coast**, see page 72

The eastern section of Madeira is not as mountainous as the centre, but it has some wonderful coastal spots, a handful of attractive small towns, productive agricultural fields and a long, surreal promontory that juts out into the Atlantic.

As you head out of Funchal, the village of **Santo da Serra** ⓰, popular for its Sunday morning farmers' market, can be reached via Camacha or from the Poiso crossroads. The altitude of 670 metres (2,200ft) produces refreshing breezes, and explains why several wealthy British expats have chosen to build *quintas* here and why so many affluent Madeirans still flee the Funchal summer up into these hills.

The most striking feature of Santo da Serra is its flatness; it may not be in the league of Paúl da Serra, but it is still large enough to accommodate a 27-hole golf course (see page 82). Even if you're not much of a golfer, you might still enjoy a stroll through the pleasant gardens of **Quinta da Junta** (free), once owned by the ubiquitous Blandy family, but now open to the public. A lookout point provides views across to Machico on the coast, and you can enjoy a drink at the golf-club bar, set in what was once a *pousada*.

LEVADA TRAILS

Few man-made things on Madeira can rival its natural gifts. *Levadas* – simple irrigation channels with paths beside them, providing direct access to the best of the island's natural beauty – offer the best of both worlds. Cut no more than 50cm (20 in) wide, and set 30–60cm (1–2ft) into the ground, *levadas* run more than 2,100km (1,300 miles) around Madeira and have been here almost as long as the island has been settled. The footpaths alongside each *levada,* built for maintenance purposes, create a great network for exploring the interior of the island. Some *levadas* are suitable for people of all ages; the only requirements are reasonable footwear, a route map (available from www.visitmadeira.com) or reliable guidebook (Sunflower Books), and, perhaps, a taxi waiting at the other end. As *levadas* wind through the hillsides, most gradients are gentle, but paths that follow the lie of the hillside can also give rise to unexpected vertiginous drops.

At **Portela** (662 metres/2,172ft), the views of the coast are striking. You may see hang-gliders taking off from a nearby platform. **Penha d'Águia** dominates the northeast coast. This huge rock formation, towering at 590 metres (1,935ft), levels off to a flat top. The name, meaning Eagle Rock, is derived from the eagles that once nested on ledges in its craggy cliff face.

The village of **Porto da Cruz**, 6km (4 miles) north, lies in the shadow of the rock and is famous for surfing and sugar cane. It has one of Madeira's few remaining sugar mills, pumping out steam as it processes the sugar cane to make *aguardente*, the local liquor, and molasses, which you can buy here.

Machico

Machico ⓱ was Madeira's first settlement, founded on the spot where João Gonçalves Zarco first came ashore in 1419. Zarco ruled the southwestern half of Madeira, while his fellow Portuguese captain and navigator, Tristão Vaz Teixeira, governed the northeastern half from Machico. A statue of Teixeira stands outside the town's fifteenth-century parish church, **Igreja Matriz**. King Manuel I donated its statue of the Virgin, the original of which is in Funchal's Sacred Art Museum.

From Machico's cobbled church square, it's a short stroll to **Praia da Banda d'Além**, a hugely popular beach of golden Moroccan sand with a picturesque marina beyond, and the landscaped seafront, home to a small custard-yellow fortress, built in 1706. Its battered walls contrast starkly with the ultramodern glass and concrete **Fórum Machico** cultural centre nearby, home to cinmas and an exhibition space. At the south end of the bay is the tiny eighteenth-century **Capela de São Roque**, while the modern suspension

Santana's unusual palheiros are unique to the area

bridge on the left of the bay leads to the **Capela dos Milagres** (Chapel of Miracles) built over the graves of Robert Machim and Anne d'Arfet, the first to set foot on Madeira (see page 22).

The northeast coast

The landscape of the extreme eastern peninsula, known as **Ponta de São Lourenço**, is more like Porto Santo (see page 74) and the Ilhas Desertas (see page 9) than Madeira. Keen walkers enjoy this wild, windswept tip of the island (Route PR8 Vereda da Ponta de São Lourenço; https://simplifica.madeira.gov.pt; charge) but, for all its wonderful views, the breezes can be a bit too invigorating for comfort.

Ponta de São Lourenço

Close by, at **Prainha**, is the island's only natural sandy beach. Not surprisingly for a volcanic island, the sand here is black; the tiny beach can be crowded in high summer, but is deserted the rest of the year.

Nearby **Caniçal** ⓲ was once a whaling port, but since whaling was banned here in 1981, all that remains of this formerly lucrative industry is a museum and souvenirs on sale around the town. The founder of the **Museu da Baleia da Madeira** (Whale Museum; www.museudabaleia.org; charge) is the epitome of a hunter-turned-gamekeeper. Once commander of the Caniçal whaling station and thus responsible for taking 100–200 of the great creatures each year, he now devotes his energy to protecting the whales and other marine life of the area. The 14-metre (45ft) model of the sperm whale is a reminder of the leviathans that once swam in great schools in the waters off Madeira. Whales are still sighted here, but far less frequently. Caniçal remains a working fishing port, and has a selection of good fish restaurants.

Heading southwest towards Funchal from Caniçal and Machico, the VR1 highway passes under the runway of the international airport, supported on huge pillars. Beyond the airport is the pleasant town of **Santa Cruz** ⓳, with an attractive church dating from 1500. Across the main square, the town hall retains a pair of splendid sixteenth-century Manueline windows.

A few streets away, the courthouse is another historic survivor, with fine verandas and an impressive main staircase. On the seafront is the modern municipal market and a pebbly beach, while to the west of the town is the island's only waterpark, the **AquaParque** (www.aquamadeira.com; charge), with slides, flumes and wave pools.

The main road along the coast towards Funchal passes **Caniço** ⓴, with an imposing eighteenth-century church and a pretty garden suburb of holiday villas and hotels, with a steep path down to a tiny beach. Merging with Caniço to the west is **Ponta do Garajau**, a holiday development popular with German visitors.

The road ends at a fine *miradouro*, where a statue of Christ stands with arms outstretched. There is also a splendid view west to the Bay of Funchal. The offshore waters are a marine protected area, the **Reserva Natural Parcial do Garajau**, making this area a great starting point for scuba diving trips.

The road dropping down into Funchal winds past some of the town's smartest villas. The first landmark is the church of São Gonçalo in the parish of the same name; photographers love this spot for its classic views down to Funchal harbour. Also in the vicinity is a tiny, atmospheric chapel, dedicated to Nossa Senhora das Neves (Our Lady of the Snows).

Porto Santo

Highlights

- **Vila Baleira**, see page 75
- **An island tour**, see page 77

The island of Porto Santo, 40km (25 miles) northeast of Madeira, is the only other inhabited island in the archipelago, with a population of around 5,200. As desert islands go, it's not exactly undiscovered – it is accessible via a 2.5-hour ferry crossing, or a very short (15min) flight – but only a handful of foreign visitors find these shores. Porto Santo is still, at heart, the resort of Madeirans, who seek what they have not: sand.

Porto Santo's prize is a 9km (6 mile) stretch of golden beach. Elsewhere, such an asset would have inspired a flurry of swish villas, boutique hotels and beach bars to be built, but so far, cutting-edge tourist and residential developments have largely eluded Porto Santo. The island is mostly quiet, apart from its three-month summer season. Out of season, even the main town seems deserted, as is the interior, with its scorched expanses and rust-coloured rock formations.

The frequently rough sea crossing (the return crossing is never as bad) drops passengers at Porto de Abrigo, on the eastern tip of the island. From the dock it is a short taxi or bus ride, or alternatively a 20-minute walk, to reach **Vila Baleira** ㉑ (sometimes referred to as **Porto Santo Town**), the island's only settlement of notable size.

Vila Baleira

The centre of Vila Baleira is a small, palm-shaded plaza, comprising a little town hall and a church that has now been restored after more than three centuries of use. **Nossa Senhora da Piedade** (Our Lady of Piety) was originally founded just after the island's discovery in the early to mid-fifteenth century. The present church was rebuilt after pirates destroyed the original in 1667, though part of it, the Morgada chapel, did survive.

Porto Santo's claim to fame, beyond its sandy beach, is its connection with Christopher Columbus. The town's major attraction is a fifteenth century house, built from rough-hewn stone, that stands next to the church, set back a little off the square: the **Casa Colombo – Museu do Porto Santo e dos Descobrimentos Portugueses** (Columbus House Museum of Porto Santo and the Portuguese Discoveries; https://cultura.madeira.gov.pt; charge). This small museum's displays

Mural, Santa Cruz market hall

include period pieces, memorabilia, replicas, maps, paintings and sketches. Tantalisingly, however, it has no personal effects belonging to Columbus himself – even his portraits are based on imagination, since no reliable likeness has survived.

The story of Columbus and the Madeiran archipelago is not entirely apocryphal, unlike so many other tales related to the islands. Columbus did marry Felipa Moniz Perestrelo, the granddaughter of the first governor of Porto Santo, Bartolomeu Perestrelo, but there is no strong evidence that this building was ever his home. That does not stop the museum claiming that Columbus lived here from 1478 to 1480 and that his tragically short-lived son, Diego, was born a *Portosantense* in this house.

The liveliest street in Vila Baleira – liveliest being a relative term – is Rua João Gonçalves Zarco, situated on the other side of the river from the plaza, running down to the sea. The street is home to a handicraft centre, and old-fashioned shops and bars, full of character. The main square is Largo do Pelourinho (Pillory Square), where, as the name indicates, local offenders were once punished.

PROPHETS AND MAGICAL SANDS

The inhabitants of Porto Santo are sometimes referred to by Madeirans as *profetas* (prophets) – the result of a strange episode in the sixteenth century, when a local shepherd started a religious cult. Not only did he claim to be able to predict the future, he held people in sway by saying he had the power to list their most intimate secrets and sins. The cult was short-lived, however, and the *Portosantenses* resumed normality. In retaliation, they sometimes call Madeirans *villões* (villains), a play on words that derives from *vila*, meaning town.

Powers of a different kind are attributed to the island's beach, which is said to hold curative properties that alleviate all kinds of aches and pains. Many Madeirans are convinced of its benefits and bury themselves up to their necks in sand.

Portela's windmills

An island tour

Porto Santo is tiny – less than 11km (6 miles) by 6km (4 miles). It does not require much sightseeing, which is good, because most people just come to bake on the beach. Hiring a car is expensive, and what there is to see is usually near the main roads.

Taxis will take you around the island, giving their own tours at fixed prices (see page 138).

Heading around the island in an anticlockwise direction, the first stop is the lookout point of **Portela** (163 metres/535ft). The most emblematic natural viewpoint in the region, it offers a panorama of the whole 9km (5.6 miles) of golden, sandy beach. Head north, however, and the desolate nature of the landscape is inescapable. Crop yields are poor, partly because of the chronic lack of water, and land that was once tended is now deserted. For most people, earning a living from tourism is more appealing than toiling away in the fields.

The island's highest peak, at 517 metres (1,695ft), is **Pico do Facho** ㉒, situated around 1.5km (1 mile) due north of Portela. You will need to don hiking boots to get to the summit. Its name, which means Peak of the Torch, derives from the warning beacons that were lit here in the days when French and Algerian pirates posed a threat to the island.

A minor road heads west out of the scattered village of **Camacha** to **Fonte da Areia** (Sand Spring), where the rugged coastline is particularly lovely. Sandstone cliffs and rocks have been weathered into interesting shapes and small caves. A spring filtering through the rocks is the source of the island's mineral water, said to guarantee eternal youth.

Porto Santo's idyllic beach

The main road continues its loop, almost bringing you back to Vila Baleira, before a minor road heads north again towards **Pico do Castelo**. It is only a couple of hundred metres from Pico do Facho, and from its height of 437 metres (1,433ft), accessible by car, it provides a commanding view itself.

Porto Santo's airport, which was much larger than the one on Madeira before the latter was expanded, lies just below; beyond it is the vivid green of Porto

Exploring Calhau da Serra on a quad bike

Santo's golf course, contrasting with the tawny hues of the rest of the island.

There are plenty of pretty places around to enjoy a picnic, such as **Morenos**, in the southwest. Neat and well-tended with plenty of sunshades, flowers and seats, it enjoys a picturesque view over to the little **Ilhéu de Ferro** (Isle of Iron).

The southernmost viewpoint is **Pico das Flores**, at 184 metres (603ft). Directly below is the southern end of Porto Santo's main beach and the island's southwest tip, **Ponta da Calheta**. While the rest of the beach is an uninterrupted expanse, backed by attractive but slightly featureless dunes, in this southwestern section there are small bays with rocky outcrops to be found. You can also enjoy a beautiful view which stretches across to the Ilhéu de Baixo. It makes a fantastic afternoon of exploring.

Carnaval celebrations in Funchal

Things to do

Outdoor activities and sports

While Madeira has no beaches to speak of, and scarcely enough flat ground for a playing surface, it offers plenty of opportunities for active holiday-makers: particularly those who enjoy walking, hiking, climbing and golf.

Walking & hiking

Mountainous Madeira, with its network of *levada* trails (see page 70), is perfect for walkers of all ages and abilities. Such water-courses exist elsewhere, but nowhere are they so accessible nor do they cover such a great area. The island's irrigation system is composed of some 2,100km (1,300 miles) of channels. The narrow paths that run alongside them are mostly gentle but exhilarating at the same time; many of them follow the contours of steep ravines, cloaked in lush, mossy laurisilva forest, or lead through inspiring highland scenery. As well as the levada paths, there are waymarked coastal routes and mountain trails, some of which follow dizzying ridges.

Official hiking routes are waymarked with PR (Pequena Rota, Short Route) numbers and their Portuguese names, with locals usually referring to them by the latter. There are useful route maps and descriptions on the Madeira Promotion Bureau website, www.visitmadeira.com. To help maintain the trails and reduce overcrowding, non-Madeiran walkers must pre-book a permit before setting out. Each slot costs €3, payable online via the Bilhética (Ticketing): Pagamento de Taxas para Percursos Pedestres Classificados section of Madeira's Simplifica portal (https://simplifica.madeira.gov.pt). From time to time, some routes are closed for repairs. For further details, visit the website of the Instituto das Florestas e da Conservação da Natureza (Forest and Nature Conservation Institute, IFCN; https://ifcn.madeira.gov.pt/en).

The most popular and beautiful levada trails include **PR6.1 Levada do Risco** (moderate; 4hr there-and-back) **PR9 Levada do Caldeirão Verde** (moderate; 6.5hr). Recommended mountain and coastal routes include the following: **PR12 Caminho Real da Encumeada** (moderate; 5hr): views of Curral das Freiras and Ribeiro do Poco valley. **PR1 Vereda do Areeiro and PR 1.2 Vereda do Pico Ruivo** (moderate–difficult; 5hr): an epic hike to Madeira's highest peaks, Areeiro, Torres and Ruivo, ending at Achada do Teixeira. **PR8 Vereda da Ponta de São Lourenço** (moderate; 5hr there-and-back): great rock formations, flora and views of the Atlantic.

All these can be undertaken alone by experienced walkers or with local guides (see page 132), but it is best to know in advance what you are likely to encounter and a reliable walkers' guidebook (see page 136) is a good investment.

The footpaths alongside levadas make great walking trails

Golf

This is a year-round sport on Madeira. The islands' three courses are esteemed for their scenic beauty. Having staged the Madeira Island Open on numerous occasions (part of the PGA European Tour), the 27-hole **Clube de Golf Santo da Serra** (www.santodaserragolf.com) is one of Europe's most exciting championship courses, suitable for all levels. Designed by Robert Trent Jones, the course is close to the picturesque village of Santo da Serra, east of Funchal, and has stupendous views to the sea below. **Palheiro Golf** (www.palheirogolf.com) is in the São Gonçalo hills, 15 minutes east of the centre of Funchal. The course, designed by Cabell Robinson, has 18 holes and is set on the Palheiro Nature Estate. So spectacular are the views over the bay and city that it is a great place to visit, even if you don't play golf. On Porto Santo, **Porto Santo Golfe** (www.portosantogolfe.com) is an 18-hole course designed by Seve Ballesteros, located in a green valley on the slopes of the Pico Ana Ferreira mountain, with sea breezes and coastal scenery.

NOTES

If you are going to do some of Madeira's serious walking trails, take warm layers and waterproofs, as the weather can change very abruptly. Hiking boots with good support and traction are a sensible idea to combat uneven or loose surfaces, and sunblock is essential.

Swimming

Although much of Madeira's coast drops dizzily into the sea, offering little or no safe access for bathers, there is an artificial beach with imported golden sand at Calheta (and Machico), and a number of **lido complexes and natural swimming pools** around the coast with showers, toilets, lifeguards and cafés, along with concrete jetties that lead out to safe sea bathing and diving areas. Among the best are those in Porto Moniz, Seixal, Ponta Delgada, Ponta Gorda and Porto da Cruz. For something more natural, there is the small black-sand beaches at Prainha and Seixal and the bathing complex east of São Jorge. Alternatively, you can enjoy slides and flumes at Santa Cruz's **Aquaparque** (see page 73); though rather small, it's fun for kids.

There are man-made sandy beaches in Machico and Calheta, but for the real thing, beach lovers should hop islands to the 9km (6 miles) of sand at **Porto Santo** (though sunshine is only really guaranteed between June and August). To get there, fly with TAP Air Portugal (15min flight) or take the daily ferry at 8am (www.portosantoline.pt).

Most of the good hotels have swimming pools and Funchal's Hotel Zone has a year-round public open-air swimming pool, the **Complexo Balnear do Lido** (Lido Swimming Complex; www.frentemarfunchal.pt). There are two main pools, plus a children's pool, sunbathing along the terraces and rocks by the sea, and catering facilities. What's more, it's cheap. Other options include **Complexo Balnear da Barreirinha**, for sea swimming near the **São Tiago Fortress**, and the excellent, indoor **Funchal Olympic Swimming Pool Complex** (www.anatacaodamadeira.pt).

A lido complex in Porto da Cruz

Sail, paddle and board sports

Funchal and Calheta's marinas offer a wealth of boat charters and excursions. The calm but breezy south coast of Madeira and the clear, shallow waters off Porto Santo are also ideal for sea kayaking, stand-up paddleboarding, windsurfing and kitesurfing. For surfing, Madeira's most formidable waves pound the shore at Jardim do Mar and Pául do Mar in the southwest; if you're a beginner, you're better off joining the local boardriders at Porto da Cruz in the east or São Vicente in the north.

Tennis

Flat land is at such a premium in Funchal that even the likes of Reid's Palace and the Royal Savoy can only afford two tennis courts each. There are four at Funchal's Quinta Magnólia sports centre (https://simplifica.madeira.gov.pt; charge).

Trail running

The island's *levadas* and mountain paths are a true paradise for trail runners, who can participate in several competitions throughout the year, including the prestigious Madeira Island Ultra Trail (www.miutmadeira.com). The most challenging MIUT category is a hefty 115km (70-mile) course with steep climbs, varied terrain and unpredictable weather conditions – not for the faint of heart.

Scuba diving

Divers are in luck in the Madeira Islands, since one of Europe's first underwater nature protected areas, the Garajau Partial Nature Reserve, was created along the Garajau coastline. Besides abundant, colourful fish, divers can see shipwrecks. Sea temperatures vary between 18° and 24°C (64 and 75°F). Several diving schools are recommended. **Manta Diving Centre** (www.mantadiving.com), based in Caniço east along the coast from Funchal, offers wreck-, night-, cave- and Nitrox-diving. **Focus Natura** (www.focusnatura.

Diving is popular on Madeira

com) based in Santa Cruz offers everything from beginners' courses and single dives to advanced tuition. Alternatively, the **Madeira Dive Point** (www.madeiradivepoint.com) at the Pestana Carlton Madeira Hotel offers diving equipment for hire, and various courses.

Wildlife-watching

Madeira offers superb nature-focused boat trips lasting from a couple of hours to a full day, on which you're highly likely to see dolphins and whales (sperm whales can be seen all year) and a host of seabirds. With luck, manta rays and loggerhead turtles can be sighted, too. Land-based spotters help guide the boats: they scan the ocean from the clifftops, looking for tell-tale bird activity and plumes of spray. An impressive 356 bird species have been recorded in the archipelago, including four endemic species, and a few more found only in Macaronesia (the Azores, Madeira, Canary and Cape Verde). Good birding areas include the central highlands, the laurisilva forests on the mountains' northern slopes, and the western and eastern extremities, Ponta do Pargo and Ponta de São Lourenço.

Cycling

Madeira has some thrilling long-distance road cycling routes that immerse you in the islands' rugged rural landscapes. Off road, there are world-class mountain biking trails to tackle: a scenic experience, if you're brave enough to look up. Specialist outfits such as Freeride (www.freeridemadeira.com) lead rides, organise events and keep the trails in tiptop condition.

Extreme sports

With sheer cliffs, gullies and gushing waterfalls carved by long-ago volcanic activity, Madeira is an adventure playgrounds for intrepid adventurers. Canyoning and coasteering – descending mountain rivers or exploring rocky coastlines by jumping, sliding, abseiling and swimming, with dramatic cliffs, lush ferns and mosses all around – are best tackled in a group with expert guides, who will start by kitting you out with a wetsuit, helmet and shoes. On Madeira, the most popular canyoning locations are Ribeira da Hortelã near Porto Moniz and Ribeira Funda near Seixal, with their glorious waterfalls, and Ribeira do Lajeado near Rabaçal, a 1.9km canyoning trail that will takes a little over four hours to complete. There are half a dozen other spots, mostly on the north coast. Ponta de São Lourenço is excellent for coasteering.

Horse riding

Lessons and cross-country riding are offered by the **Associação Hípica da Madeira** at Quinta Villa Alpires, just outside Funchal. Horse riding can also be arranged at **Quinta do Riacho** (www.equinevillage.com) and on the island of Porto Santo at the **Centro Hípico**.

Big game fishing and boat trips

In the deep Atlantic, just beyond Madeira's shallow waters, you can catch – depending on the season – giant blue marlin, bonito, tuna (big-eye, blue-fin and yellow-fin), barracuda, swordfish, wahoo and shark (hammerhead, mako and blue). Madeira's sport-fishing companies operate a 'tag and release' scheme whereby any fish caught are returned unharmed to the wild after photographing.

The very best deep-sea fishing is from June to September. **Madeira Sight Casting** (www.madeirasightcasting.com) and Captain Peter Bristow of **Fish Madeira** (www.fishmadeira.com) run fishing expeditions that set out from Funchal Marina.

Spectator sports

The only sport to watch on Madeira is *futebol*, **football**. Islanders are wild about the game beautiful game and are devoted to their most successful teams – Maritímo (www.csmaritimo.org.pt) and Nacional (www.cdnacional.pt). Maritímo played in the Portuguese Primeira Liga from 1985 to 2023, but has since been relegated to Liga 2. Their stadium is on Rua Dr Pita. Nacional were promoted from Liga 2 to the Primeira Liga in 2024, and their stadium is high above Funchal at Choupana. The latter discovered the talent of Cristiano Ronaldo, who played for Nacional until he was 12.

Shopping

Madeira is an outstanding shopping destination, given its long craft heritage. The island is renowned for wicker items, exquisite handmade lace and embroidery, gorgeous flowers and local wines. Traditional, labour-intensive methods and quality are still respected on Madeira.

NOTES

Madeirans do not take a midday siesta, but most businesses, including shops, close for a one- or two-hour lunch break.

Best buys

Hand-stitched embroidery

Wicker

Madeira's artisans produce an outstanding array of wicker items: linen, shopping and picnic baskets, tables, chairs, trays and much more besides. The willow wicker is so strong, it is even used to make the iconic Monte sledges. Accustomed to exporting, most companies will gladly send large items to Europe and North America for you, if you don't have the luggage space.

The industry started in the 1850s in Camacha, where willow trees thrive across the wet valley, and this parish is still the wicker capital of Madeira. Wickerwork in the making is far more interesting than it sounds: items are crafted with hands and feet, and occasionally teeth as well.

Needlework

Madeira's beautiful hand embroidery and cutwork is unsurpassed. This globally disappearing art form – still going strong on Madeira – is an amalgam of styles and techniques that has evolved over more than 150 years. Along with fortified wine, embroidery and lacemaking are Madeira's superlative exports, and in Funchal you have ample opportunity to visit factories or workshops where the final touches are put to these painstakingly produced items. Madeira creates and exports table linens, sheets, dresses, blouses, handkerchiefs and even wedding dresses of extraordinary delicacy. The materials, selected for their smoothness and quality, include natural silk, linen, organdie and cotton.

If you are used to machine-made, mass-produced embroidered items, you may be in for a price-tag shock, however. A full set of meticulously detailed table linens can take up to two years to make, and is priced accordingly. To be sure that any needlework item is genuine, look for a lead seal (or a hologram) with the emblem of IVBAM. This seal confirms the piece has been certified by the Instituto do Vinho, do Bordado e do Artesanato da Madeira (Institute of Wine, Embroidery and Handicrafts of Madeira; https://ivbam.madeira.gov.pt), an official island organisation.

Traditional knitwear for sale

Other handicrafts

Though wicker and needlework are the biggest sellers, other craft items also make good souvenirs and gifts. **Boots** made from soft goatskin are part of the national costume. The boot and leather goods seller just outside the entrance of Funchal's Mercado dos Lavradores is worth a visit. The boots worn by the *carreiros*, the sled-men who push the Monte toboggans, are also available (as are the **straw boaters**, that they wear). Souvenirs with a more contemporary touch include bags and purses made from stripey Madeiran cloth, miniature hiking trail signs, hand-embroidered t-shirts and artisan soap.

Other items include **marquetry**, a revived island craft that is featured on small boxes, pictures and furniture. The **brinquinho** is Madeira's answer to the tambourine, in which miniature cymbals are clashed together by costumed dolls 'dancing' round a handheld maypole.

Ceramics and pottery such as pretty hand-painted plates, planters, jugs, jars and colourful azulejo tiles, are hugely popular, although most of the items sold on Madeira come from mainland Portugal. You will find thick **knitwear** – pullovers, hats and gloves and plenty more – at many shops up in the mountains, again, imported from the mainland.

Food and drink

Madeira cake and wine are extremely long-lasting, so you can safely bring some back home. Genuine Madeira cake, *bolo de mel* (sugar cane molasses cake, sometimes mistranslated as honey cake) is sold in many different sizes. Dating back to Madeira's hey-day of sugar manufacturing, it is very different from the British treat known as Madeira cake; it is dark, heavy, chewy and delicious, with a similar flavour to gingerbread. It lasts for at least a year and goes very well with a dry Madeira wine. You will also find plentiful supplies of traditional biscuits, honey, jams and marmalades.

Bring a bird of paradise home

A bottle or two of Madeira wine (see page 111) make excellent souvenirs or gifts. Connoisseurs with money to burn hunt down vintage bottles – you can still turn up rarities like Blandy's Bual 1920 or Henriques & Henriques' Bastardo 1927.

When buying *aguardente* (sugar cane spirit), remember that *aguardente velha* (old) is the smoothest. Other alcoholic drinks that you might want to take home include *branquinha* (*aguardente* with a stick of sugar cane in the bottle), or a local liqueur such as *licor de maracujá* (passionfruit) or *ginja* (cherry liqueur).

Flowers

Recreating a lush Madeiran garden isn't easy, but you can still take home souvenir flamingo flowers *(anthuriums)*, orchids and bird of paradise flowers (*strelitzias*, or *estrelícias* in Portuguese). The latter in particular will last quite a while after your return home. Most shops will box these for storage in the aircraft hold and deliver them either to your hotel or the airport on the day you leave. Orchid plants and flowers can be purchased all over the island at flower stands, markets and in florist shops.

Where to shop

Funchal's cathedral quarter and Old Town contain the best variety of unique shops and local products on the island. The main shopping streets are Fernão Ornelas, Ferreiros, Queimada de Cima and Queimada de Baixo. The city has transformed in recent years: large shopping centres in the Hotel Zone and elsewhere stock the major brands and ubiquitous high-street chains have sprung up alongside classic boutiques.

For needlework, visit any of Funchal's factories, which put the finishing touches on items and act principally as showrooms, selling direct to the public. Keep an eye out for outlets marked by small signs in doorways. Among the best is **Bordal** (Rua Dr. Fernão de Ornelas 77; www.bordal.pt). There are handmade items for sale at **Artesanato da Madeira** (Rua dos Ferreiros 152; https://artesanatodamadeira.pt/

Brightly costumed flower seller in Funchal's market

loja-do-artesanato), an exhibition space and shop run by IVBAM, whose embroidery website (www.bordadomadeira.com) lists other recommendations.

Wicker products are offered everywhere in Funchal – you will find one of the biggest shops in Rua do Castanheiro – and all over Madeira, but the main centre for wickerwork with the biggest choice is located in the village of Camacha. It is Madeira's 'All Things Wicker', with items ranging from the most conventional to the most implausible.

There are flower sellers along Avenida Arriaga near the Sé (Cathedral) as well as inside the **Mercado dos Lavradores** on Rua Brigadeiro Oudinot. Shops specialising in selling and packaging flowers for long-distance transport include **A Flor da Ajuda** (Rua Velha de Ajuda 5).

For Madeira wines, the most atmospheric place to shop is the **Adegas de São Francisco** (see page 37; Avenida Arriaga 28; www.blandyswinelodge.com) next to the tourist office. It has tasting rooms where you can even try vintage wines dating from 1920, a shop selling the four brands now owned by the Madeira Wine Company (Blandy's, Cossart Gordon, Miles and Leacock), a

COLOURFUL CHARACTERS

Madeiran street flower sellers wear traditional costume – not only good for business, but required by law. Ladies in cheerful garb, as colourful as the flowers they hawk, gather alongside the cathedral at the main city market.

Younger girls wear the same red and yellow striped skirts, often with a red bolero jacket and red cape, for folk-dance demonstrations. Men wear white linen trousers and white shirts, with red cummerbunds. Black skullcaps, with curly tassels like candle wicks, are worn by both men and women, as are the native *botachã* (literally, plain boots), made from tanned ox hide and goat skin. Women's boots are distinguished by a red band (see page 91).

book and souvenir shop, and a pleasant café. Other possibilities for purchasing wine in Funchal include **Pérola dos Vinhos** (Rua da Alfândega; https://loja.peroladosvinhos.com) and the city's supermarkets, which stock various brands. The winery and shop of **Henriques & Henriques**, producers of award-winning wines, is located in Câmara de Lobos (www.henriqueseh enriques.pt).

Adegas de São Francisco

If you have run out of things to read by the pool, check out **Livraria Bertrand Bookstore** (Rua Dr Brito Câmara 19 and Estrada Monumental 390; bertrand.pt) or the old-fashioned **Livraria Esperança** (Rua dos Ferreiros 156; www.livraria-esperanca.pt). Here you will discover thousands of used books, some in English.

Culture and entertainment

Funchal's **Teatro Municipal** (https://teatrobaltazardias.funchal.pt) is the only place that regularly stages theatrical shows and concerts. It is worth a visit, if only to see the theatre itself. Dating from 1888, it has been restored to its original splendour, and produces most of the performing arts. It is the centrepiece of the annual **Atlantic Festival** held in June. This festival attracts some of the big names in the classical music world, and the best of the concerts are broadcast on the island's radio station.

Throughout the year, students and teachers from the Madeira Music Conservatoire perform at atmospheric venues such as the Quinta das Cruzes museum (see page 43). Visit the tourist office on Avenida Arriaga for further concert information.

For an authentic taste of Portugal, two places offer regular *fado* evenings. These are **Arsénio's** restaurant (Rua de Santa Maria 169; www.grupocafedoteatro.com) and **Sabor a Fado** (Travessa das Torres 10; www.saborafado.webnode.pt), where even the waitresses can sing fado. Wailing *fado* songs, accompanied by classical guitar, generally deal with the hardships of love and life. Folk-dancing evenings are a regular feature at hotels and local tour companies will arrange folklore evenings at a restaurant where some of Madeira's very best dancers give a performance.

Sabor a Fado

Festivals

Madeira has a busy calendar of religious, secular and cultural festivals, some of which were devised relatively recently with the main aim of entertaining visitors. As inauthentic as that may sound, the locals have taken them to heart, making them hugely successful and great fun. The biggest events are Carnival, the Flower Festival, Wine Festival and New Year's Eve. As long as you don't mind crowds, these can be the best time to visit the island. Popular additions to

Funchal's Flower Festival

the calendar include the Atlantic Festival in June, a 23-day summer celebration with fireworks, circus shows and food events, and the Nature Festival in October, which combines hikes and boat trips with outdoor concerts, and Whale Festival. Every island community also has its own small-scale local festival, known as an arrial, featuring live music, food and drink.

Carnival

Staged in February (occasionally in March), the pre-Lenten **Carnaval** (Carnival) is celebrated in the streets of Funchal with Brazilian-style samba rhythms. Each year this parade is assigned an overall creative theme. Though nowhere near as hedonistic and extravagant as, say, the Rio carnival, this is a colourful and vibrant multi-day celebration.

Fireworks over Funchal's harbour during the Atlantic Festival

Flower Festival

The **Festa da Flor**, held in late April or early May, is a crowd-pleaser. Floats – decorated in beautiful, inventive floral creations – parade through Funchal's streets. There's a **children's parade**, in which each child carries a single flower and places it in a hole in a 'Wall of Hope' in the Praça do Município. Once the parades are finished, an **exhibition** of the award-winning displays is staged in a lovely old house in Rua dos Castanheiros.

Wine Festival

The Festa do Vinho commences at the end of August in wine villages, such as Estreito de Câmara de Lobos, to celebrate the September harvest. You may occasionally see grapes being crushed the traditional way: barefoot men and women treading the grapes. Wine samples are also served from traditional goatskin bags once used to store and carry wine. Funchal joins in with a pop-up wine lounge and music stage in Praça do Povo.

New Year's Eve

Madeira's biggest and most spectacular festival has an international reputation. Every year, Funchal's hotels are packed, with guests booking many months in advance and paying a hefty premium. Several winter cruise ships anchor in Funchal harbour on 31 December to participate in the party. At midnight, all the houses in town switch on all their lights, opening all the doors and windows, setting the hillside ablaze with light. The cruise ships crank up their floodlights, and the parties begin. As the New Year rings in, a splendid and exciting fireworks display erupts.

Religious festivals

Several **religious festivals** also take place throughout the year, but one especially stands out – the Festival of **Nossa Senhora do Monte** (Our Lady of Monte) is celebrated on 15 August, the **Feast of the Assumption**, in Monte. Pilgrims flock from all around the island to kiss the image of the patron saint, and some ascend the final 68 steps to the church on their knees.

To the many Madeirans who believe that the Lady of Monte has carried them through troubled times, the pilgrimage is an obligation. The sick and infirm arrive in droves in search of miraculous cures. Alongside the pious devotions, wine flows, fireworks explode and *espetada* (kebab) stalls flourish, before Monte regains normality for another year.

Nightlife

Madeira's after-dark entertainment scene is very low-key compared to, say, the Balearic or Canary Islands. Funchal has plenty of bars plus a handful of nightclubs and even a well-attended casino with revues, but the majority of visitors do not come to the island in search of a hedonistic nightlife, preferring to do as the locals do – chat over dinner and drinks. The closest the island gets to a party vibe is when cool bars and hotels in Funchal and hotspots such as Calheta and Porto da Cruz hire DJs for sunset cocktail sessions.

The nucleus of the tourist-nightlife scene consists mainly of the major hotels and their bars and nightclubs. At Funchal's **Casino da Madeira** (Avenida do Infante; www.casinodamadeira.com) in the grounds of the Pestana Casino Park hotel, you can play blackjack, roulette and slot machines, or soak up the for the *tropicália* vibes at **Copacabana** (https://casinodamadeira.com/discoteca), **a club** with live bands and DJs sets. The other principal hotel for nightlife is the Pestana Carlton Madeira (www.pestana.com), which has a casino and nightclub, and puts on themed evenings as well as classical concerts and children's shows.

The bars on Rua da Alfândega and Rua das Fontes in Funchal city centre and Rua de Santa Maria in the Zona Velha burst at the seams at weekends. Young people also head for the **Café do Teatro** (Avenida Arriaga, next to the theatre; www.grupocafedoteatro.com), a chic city-centre bar with an elegant interior and pavement tables; the staff rig up an outfood screen whenever there's a big football match. Other popular spots in the heart of Funchal include the city's poncha bars, such as **Madeira Rum House** (Rua Portão de São Tiago 19; www.madeirarumhouse.com), **FugaCidade** (Rua do Conde de Cannavial 22), a laidback little bar that's brilliant for Portuguese craft beer and cider, **Revolucion** (Rua do Sabão 82) a feisty bar run by fanatical mixologists, and the wine bar **O Americano** (Rua da Carreira 120). Cocktail bar **23 Vintage** (Rua Santa Maria 23) has good vibes and DJs bringing back the spirit of the 1970s, 1980s and 1990s. For excellent, wallet-friendly drinks head to **Hole in One** at Estrada Monumental 238A in the Hotel Zone; it has a lovely garden under banana trees.

Funchal nightlife

Calendar of events

5 January *Festa dos Reis/Cantar os Reis* (Sing of the Kings): Funchal and elsewhere.

15 January *Santo Amaro Festival* and close of Christmas festivities.

Late January *São Sebastião* celebrated in Caniçal and Câmara de Lobos.

February/March *Carnaval*: huge festival in Funchal, culminating in a colourful procession on the Saturday before Shrove Tuesday (see page 97).

May *Festa da Flor* (Flower Festival): floral floats parade through Funchal, also the Children's Parade and Wall of Hope (see page 98).

June *Festival do Atlântico* (Atlantic Festival): weekend musical performances in Funchal's Teatro Municipal and other venues, and firework displays over the harbour.

23–24 June *São João da Ribeira* (Feast of St John) celebrated in Funchal, São João, Câmara de Lobos, Ponta do Sol and elsewhere.
29 June *São Pedro* (St Peter), patron saint of fishermen: bonfires and boat procession at Ribeira Brava, Ponta do Pargo and Cãmara de Lobos.
1 July *Dia da Madeira* (Madeira Day): Madeirans celebrate political autonomy from Portugal. Events across Madeira.
Mid-July *Funchal Jazz Festival*: top musicians perform in the Jardim Municipal and Parque de Santa Catarina (www.funchaljazz.com)
Mid-July *Festa da Cereja* (Cherry Festival) in Jardim da Serra, Câmara de Lobos: a weekend of sport and culture to celebrate the cherry harvest.

Folk dancers in Funchal

Late July *24 Horas a Bailar*: 24-hour folk-dance marathon, Santana.

14–15 August *Festa da Nossa Senhora do Monte* (Our Lady of Monte): pilgrims flock to Monte from all around the island.

25 August–11 September *Festa do Vinho* (Madeira Wine Festival): grape harvesting in Estreito de Câmara de Lobos and other areas, with shows and exhibitions here and in Funchal.

Mid-September *Festival Columbo*, Porto Santo: music concerts and street parades celebrate the great navigator.

Festa do Vinho

Early October *Festival da Baleia* (Madeira Whale Fest): Live music, exhibitions and events in Funchal and Caniçal.

October *Festival da Natureza* (Madeira Nature Festival): adventure and cultural activities for all ages.

October *Festival de Órgão da Madeira* (Madeira Organ Festival), Funchal: 10-day musical feast.

1 November Parade and performances for *Festa da Castanha* (Chestnut Festival) in Curral das Freiras.

November Madeira Street Arts Festival: pop-up performances including circus, dance and music in Funchal over three days, with the fourth day at Calheta waterfront.

December Christmas illuminations in Funchal from 1 December and fireworks on New Year's Eve.

Food and drink

Funchal has been catering for visitors since Victorian times. While it's not Portugal's dining capital, there are plenty of good restaurants, the finest of which have Michelin stars. In recent years, there's been a surge of interest in ultra-local ingredients and artisan drinks, from craft cider, rum and gin to small-batch coffee, and international-style ad hoc eating has taken off, with food trucks and pop-up bars appearing in Funchal's Praça do Povo and other event spaces.

Top 10 things to try

Madeira has its own typical dishes, in addition to Portuguese specialities. As a rule, the food here is simple; it uses fresh ingredients and is served up in hearty portions.

1. Bolo do caco

A Madeiran trademark, this excellent bread is made from wheat and sweet potato, and often served with garlic butter *(manteiga de alho)*. It has a thin crust with a light centre, making the texture both fluffy and crisp – a result of baking directly on a hot surface. The origin of this slightly sweet, round bread if believed to be from Arab influence, as far back as the 15th century.

2. Sopa de tomate e cebola com ovo

Soup is always on the menu and the best is usually Madeira's *own*, a delicious blend of tomatoes and onions, served with a poached egg floating on top. The ultimate comfort food and a staple for vegetarians, the lively flavours come from a mix of garlic and summer herbs. The meal is often served with rustic bread.

NOTES

Salt and pepper are not usually placed on the table. But you will be given them if you ask: *sal e pimenta, faz favor.*

The fearsome-looking espadas

3. Lapas grelhadas

The island's limpets taste meatier than mussels (some of them taste almost like liver) and are served grilled in the shell. Other local seafood favourites are *polvo* (octopus), served cold in a salad or hot, fried or stewed; and *lulas* (squid), grilled, fried or stuffed (*recheado*). Shellfish do not flourish in Madeiran waters, and all prawns and lobsters are imported.

4. Espadarte fumado

The pricey Portuguese delicacy of smoked swordfish is a little like smoked salmon, but tastes less sweet and has a slightly coarser texture. It's served as a starter in upmarket restaurants, often accompanied by tropical-flavoured sides, such as banana and a passionfruit sauce.

5. Espada con banana

Madeira's speciality fish, seen on menus across the island, is the *espada. Not to be confused with espadarte (swordfish) or espetada (kebab)*, this is a fearsome-looking, ink-black, eel-like beast, which can grow to around 1 metre (3ft) in length and has long, needle-sharp teeth. Despite its nasty appearance, it has delicious white meat. Some restaurants serve it poached, but more often fillets are fried and topped with a banana, which complements the flavour surprisingly well.

6. Bife de atum

The other fish that's common in these parts is tuna (*atum*), often served as a steak (*bife*) with a Madeira-wine sauce (*a Madeirense*). Maize or cornmeal (*milho*) deep-fried in cubes (also an island speciality) is the standard accompaniment to this and many other meals in rustic restaurants around the island. Other fish you may see on the menu, usually grilled or fried, include *pargo* and *besugo*, which are types of sea bream; *garoupa* and *cherne*, types of grouper; *bodião* (parrot-fish); and *bacalhau*, the famous salt-cod, cooked in many different ways. It is often served in a casserole, which tends to hide its distinctive, preserved flavour. Try it *cozido* (boiled).

7. Caldeirada

This rich stew is made from fish, potato, tomato and onion. Other slow-simmering Portuguese favourites that often appear on restaurant menus include *cataplana*, a mixture of ingredients such as clams, ham, sausage, onion, garlic, parsley, white wine and paprika, named after the copper pressure cooker it's cooked in.

8. Espetada

Not to be confused with *espada* or *espadarte*, *espetada* is the typical Madeiran meat dish, a kebab of barbecued beef, traditionally threaded on a skewer of sweet bay. In many restaurants, however,

The breathtaking view from the terrace at Villa Cipriani

a metal skewer with a hook on one end is used, and hung vertically from a stand fixed to your dining table. The beef is marinated in garlic and wine to make it tender and tasty – though it can occasionally still be tough. For something easier on the jaw, try pork in wine and garlic (*porco de vinho e alho*), which is marinated, tenderised and then grilled. Chicken (*frango*) is always on the menu, and may be served plain, grilled, African-style (as in *piri-piri*, when it's basted in a sauce of hot chilli peppers, then grilled) or in a Goan-inspired curry sauce. Ox tongue (*língua*) served with Madeira-wine sauce is also a Portuguese speciality.

9. Pudim de maracuja

This creamy, fruity mousse is hugely popular, as is *pudim de leite* (milk pudding) and *gelado* (ice cream). Restaurants may also offer

NOTES

Most restaurants serve a *couvert*, an assortment of appetisers, including bread and butter, which arrive unasked. You will be charged anything from €1 to €5 for the items. If you do not touch them, however, you should not, in theory, be charged for them.

seasonal fruit after your meal, since the island has an excellent range of exotic fruits. Sample them fresh from the market if not in a restaurant: a favourite is *anonas* or custard apple (originally from Peru). Split in half, the flesh is soft and white, with large black pips. Other popular desserts include *malassadas* (a deep-fried yeast dough served with sugar cane honey)

10. Bolo de mel (molasses cake)

A delicately spiced, chewy cake made with local sugar cane molasses, *bolo de mel* is traditionally torn apart, rather than cut. It pairs beautifully with tea or Madeira wine. Another favourite treat is *queijada*, a small sweet tart with a baked egg and curd cheese filling (see page 105).

Where and when to eat

For international or haute cuisine, most the best places are in the hotel zone and the up-market, far end of the Old Town. Some of the smarter restaurants are rather formal, with tablecloths, a dress code and a hushed atmosphere. If you would prefer a more authentically Madeiran, local experience, try the side streets around the cathedral, Rua Carreira or cafés along Rua Dom Carlos I. Alternatively, ask any local guides and hotel staff you get to know about their favourite off-the-beaten-track places, and jump in a cab.

For breakfast *(pequeno almoço)*, most Madeirans start their day with toast or a sweet pastry and coffee. Hotels usually serve the standard international buffet, with bacon and eggs, cold meat, cheese, fruit and cereals. Most Madeiran restaurants stick to traditional opening times, with lunch *(almoço)* served from around noon to 3pm and dinner *(jantar)* from 7 to 10pm. However, many restaurants in Funchal offer all-day service, not closing after lunch, and you will never have any problems finding cafés serving snacks all day.

Food and drink tours are increasingly popular, and a great way to tune in your taste buds. You'll spend a few hours with a guide, visiting Funchal's inspiring Mercado dos Lavradores, learning about local specialities and tasting samples from selected bars, bakeries, delis and restaurants.

Bolo de mel

Table wines

Table wines in Madeira represent a recent history, about three decades old. There are various varieties of Madeiran table wine, of which Atlantis rosé is the most famous, sold across the island. Most good restaurants stock a full complement of Portuguese wines (top restaurants will also offer foreign labels), many of which are excellent.

You need do nothing more than tell the waiter *tinto* (red) or *branco* (white), and you can't go wrong. However, several of the best wine-producing regions have names whose use is controlled by law (*denominação de origem controlada*), and it's worth seeking out wines from the best regions. Dão and Douro in the north of

Madeiran seafood skewers

Portugal produce vigorous reds and flavourful whites. Wines from the Alentejo region are also highly regarded.

Vinho Verde (literally green wine), popular all over Portugal, is named for its youth, rather than its colour, and has a slight fizz. It goes well with simple fish and seafood dishes.

The two most celebrated Portuguese wines, port and Madeira, are primarily known as dessert wines, but they may also be sipped as aperitifs. The before-dinner varieties are dry or extra dry white port, and dry or medium-dry Madeira wines (Sercial, Terrantez and Verdelho). These should be served slightly chilled. After dinner, sip one of the famous ruby or tawny ports (aged tawny is especially good) or a Madeira dessert wine (Bual and Malvasia).

Madeira wine

The history of the island's eponymous drink, famous the world over, is as full and well-rounded as a bottle of the best vintage Malvasia. When the island was first settled during the fifteenth century, Prince Henry ordered Zarco to plant vines, brought to the island from Crete. Although wine was not planned as a major export, it became one of the most important products of the island, thanks to a combination of its notable quality and Madeira's position on the shipping lanes to the East and West Indies. The island was an obvious stopping point, where water, fresh food and wine could be taken on-board. With the rise of the British colonies in North America and the West Indies, Madeira wine was soon established as a favourite on both sides of the Atlantic, and shipped all over the British Empire.

Initially, Madeira was not a fortified wine, but gradually the addition of grape brandy became common practice in order to stabilise it on long sea voyages. During the eighteenth century, it was discovered that shipping the wine actually improved its longevity as well as its flavour. Producers realised that tropical heat was the key ingredient, and towards the end of the century, pipes of Madeira

Aged bottles of Blandy's Madeira wine

were loaded as ballast on transatlantic journeys in order to 'cook' them as much as possible. When it became impractical to send barrels on return trips, conditions for heating the wine had to be reproduced at home. The easiest way was simply to store barrels in lofts that soaked up abundant sunlight. Subsequently, special tanks called *estufas*, centrally heated by hot-water pipes, were employed; this system is still in use today for cheaper Madeira wines, subjecting the wine to a temperature of 35°C (95°F) for six months.

Oxidisation during the heating process renders the wine virtually indestructible. A bottle of Madeira can be kept uncorked for many months without suffering any deterioration, even when other types of fortified wine (such as port) would moulder quickly under such conditions. For this reason, there are Madeira wines from the early 1800s that are entirely drinkable today.

Choosing a bottle. There are several types of Madeira, each named after the grape that gives that style of wine its distinctive flavour and characteristics. The lightest and driest is Sercial, which has a full-bodied, nutty flavour, not unlike an *amontillado* sherry. It is best served chilled as an aperitif. Verdelho and Terrantez are both classified as medium-dry and should be served slightly chilled. These are tangy aperitifs, and are also recommended as an accompaniment to soup. Bual, probably introduced by the Jesuits in the seventeenth century, is a rich, port-like Madeira with a splendid honeyed taste and an underlying acidity, which means that it can cut through sweet desserts and is also a good accompaniment to cheese. Finally, and most famously, Malvasia (also known as Malmsey) is the richest of all, and is usually served following a meal.

Some Madeira wines are made from blends of several years, and the skill and style of the blender is what gives the wines of different shippers their individual character. The youngest component of the blend gives the stated age of the wine on the label: Finest is a

LIQUID HISTORY

It was Shakespeare who first gave Madeira wine a literary platform, when in *Henry IV* Falstaff is accused of selling his soul for a leg of chicken and a goblet of Madeira. The real Henry IV actually died before the discovery of the island, let alone the wine. In 1478, the Duke of Clarence went one better than Falstaff and actually drowned in a barrel of Malmsey. Sir Winston Churchill was once presented with a bottle of 1792 Sercial in Reid's Hotel, then delighted his guests by placing a napkin over his arm and assuming the duties of waiter.

But Madeira wine didn't win favour with just the British. It was used to toast the American Declaration of Independence, and drunk at the Inauguration of George Washington, who was said to consume a pint of Madeira at dinner daily. Benjamin Franklin and Thomas Jefferson were also Madeira connoisseurs.

blend in which the youngest is at least 3 years old, while Reserve and Special Reserve wines are at least 5 and 10 years old, respectively. The best, however, are Vintage wines, bottled after ageing in oak casks for a minimum of 20 years.

If you really want to impress your friends back home, buy a 75ml bottle of 1875 D'Oliveiras Malvasia Madeira Family Reserve for a mere €1,000 or so. If your budget doesn't stretch to that, you can pick up more recent vintages for around €20.

Other island drinks

After Madeira, the most famous drink produced on the island is *aguardente*, a powerful sugar cane distillation, which varies in taste from virtually unpalatable firewater to smooth, aged brandy. Look for the term *velha* (old) on the label unless you have an iron constitution. Add lemon juice and honey to *aguardente* and you have *poncha*, a delicious drink that belies its ferocious base.

Bartender making poncha

Other liqueurs are distilled from the island's fruit, two notable examples being a cherry brandy from Curral das Freiras called *ginja*; and *licor de maracujá*, passion fruit liqueur (not to be confused with the soft drink, *refrigerante de maracujá*). The local Coral lager (*cerveja*) is also excellent and very welcome on a hot day.

To help you order

We'd like a table. **Queríamos uma mesa.**

I'd like a/an/some … **Queria** …

bread **pão**
rice **arroz**
butter **manteiga**
salad **salada**
coffee **um café**
soup **sopa**
dessert **sobremesa**
sugar **açucar**
fish **peixe**
tea **chá**
fruit **fruta**
wine **vinho**
ice cream **gelado**
meat **carne**
milk **leite**
fried **frito**
potatoes **batatas**
grilled **grelhado**

Menu reader

alho garlic
amêijoas baby clams
ananás pineapple
arroz rice
atum tuna
azeitonas olives
bacalhau cod (salted)
bife (vaca) steak (beef)
bolo cake
borrego lamb
camarões shrimps
caranguejo crab
cebola onion
chouriço spicy sausage
coelho rabbit
cogumelos mushrooms
empada hot pie
feijões beans
figos figs
frango chicken
gambas prawns
guisado stew
laranja orange
legumes vegetables
linguado sole
lulas squid
maçã apple
mariscos shellfish
melancia watermelon
mexilhões mussels
molho sauce
ovo egg
pimento pepper
porco pork
presunto ham
queijo cheese
robalo sea bass
sande sandwich

Places to eat

We have used the following symbols to give an idea of the price for a three-course meal for one, including wine, cover and service:

€€€€ = over 50 euros
€€€ = 30–50 euros
€€ = 20–30 euros
€ = below 20 euros

Central Funchal

Armazém do Sal Rua da Alfândega 135; www.armazemdosal.com. An unusual setting in a 400-year-old salt warehouse. Look out for the coat of arms by the door as this place isn't easy to find. A dark, rustic space, with plenty of fish and Portuguese wine on the menu. **€€€**

Art Food Corner Rua Dom Carlos I 20; www.artcaravel.com. Cheerful little café that doubles as an informal art gallery, serving healthy sandwiches, wraps and salad bowls. Daytime only. **€**

Delícia das Sopas Rua Queimada Cima 17. Handy lunchtime pitstop on a lane near the cathedral. It keeps things simple by selling cheap but filling bowls of soup, ladled out of *tureens* on the counter. They usually have fresh salads, bread and pastries, too. Daytime only. **€**

Fala Fala Arcadas São Francisco 18, Rua de São Francisco. One of the few places in Funchal that's excellent for vegetarians and vegans, this café has a short but lovely selection of falafels, tortillas, houmous and the like. Daytime only. **€**

Restaurant do Forte Forte de São Tiago; www.forte.restaurant. This place is all about the setting, atop Funchal's mustard-yellow, coastal fortress: some terrace tables here have views out to sea, through the battlements.

Expect high-quality dishes, such as rack of lamb and octopus risotto. **€€€€**

Restaurante Informal Rua Murcas 39; www.informalfoodexperience.com. In the heart of the city near the cathedral, this cosy restaurant uses seasonal ingredients of the highest quality. The weekly changing three-course set lunch is great value and very popular. There are tables outside on the quiet street. **€€€€**

Londres Rua da Carreira 64. A locals' favourite, this unpretentious Portuguese restaurant has been in business since 1976. It has a long menu of simple, well-prepared dishes such as bacalhau à brás (scrambled egg with salted cod and fried potatoes), espada and pepper steak. **€€**

Museu Café Praça Do Município 85. Prettily located on Funchal's main square, this relaxed little restaurant has a fresh, minimalist, conservatory-like vibe. There's a short, varying menu featuring excellent dishes such seasonal soup, herb-crusted fish with broccoli and seitan curry. **€€€**

Tapassol Rua Velha da Ajuda 12. Unassuming restaurant with exciting specialities such as flame-grilled pepper steak and scabbardfish flambéd in champagne. Excellent value dishes of the day. **€€**

Terra Rua Câmara Pestana 32; https://terrafoodconcept.pt. Imaginative, vegan-friendly contemporary restaurant with a healthy fine-dining menu inspired by the owners' extensive international travels. Flexibility is their trademark: if you fancy three starters or even three desserts, that's absolutely fine. The lunchtime menu is a steal. **€€**

Three House Rua Brigadeiro Oudinot 2; www.threehouse.com. This ultra-cool rooftop bar-restaurant is as good for a quick morning coffee as it is for a full lunch or evening meal. Seafood is a speciality, such as ceviche or black tiger prawns, but they also cater to vegetarians. The mood is eclectic, with North African inspired décor, Asian-Portuguese fusion cuisine and regular DJ sets generating a party vibe. **€€€**

Funchal hotel zone

Arbor Avenida do Infante 14; www.instagram.com/arbor_food_coffee. Contemporary café in a delightful garden setting. Excellent place to linger over a burger with goat's cheese or a luscious chunk of homemade banana cake with locally roasted coffee. Daytime only. **€**

Casal da Penha Rua de Penha de França 1; www.casaldapenha.com. This family-run restaurant perfectly showcases simple, regional specialities through a menu that lets the ingredients do the talking. There are tables inside, on a sheltered, flower-bedecked patio and, in summer, on the roof terrace. **€€€**

Casa Velha Rua Imperatriz Dona Amélia 69; www.casavelharestaurant.com. A formal restaurant in a conservatory-like setting with bamboo chairs, ferns, ceiling fans and a colonial feel. The short Madeiran and international menu is popular with nearby hotel guests. Piano bar downstairs. **€€€**

Desarma The Views Baía, Rua das Maravilhas 74; www.desarma.pt. This top-flight restaurant has a Michelin star for its delicate and original fare. Experienced chef Octávio Freitas, who was born in Câmara de Lobos, makes it his mission to study, cultivate and cook with organic ingredients from the island. Evenings only. **€€€€**

The Dining Room Estalagem Quinta da Casa Branca, Rua da Casa Branca 7; www.quintacasabranca.com. This sophisticated restaurant serves beautifully plated dishes, especially in its high-quality tasting menu. Decor is traditional and elegant, and there's a terrace overlooking the gardens. Dress code. **€€€€**

Dona Amélia Rua Imperatriz Dona Amélia 83; www.donaameliarestaurant.com. Views of terracotta-tiled rooftops give this charming, old-fashioned little restaurant a real sense of place. There's a well-balanced menu of simple dishes such as soup, pasta and grilled fish or meat. Evenings only. **€€€**

Il Gallo d'Oro Cliff Bay Hotel, Estrada Monumental 147; www.portobay.com. Two-Michelin starred restaurant that serves extremely sophisticated Mediterranean and Iberian cuisine under the stewardship of chef Benoît Sinthon, whose tasting menus draw culinary inspiration from Madeira's ocean, mountains and gardens. Evenings only. **€€€€**

Horta Rua de Leichlingen 11; www.portobay.com. Though it's not entirely vegetarian, plants from PortoBay's own *horta* (kitchen garden) are the stars of the show at this relaxing, contemporary restaurant, decorated with earthy, African touches. Dishes include roasted celeriac with saffron sauce, and a curry made with beluga lentils, coconut and cashews. **€€€**

William Reid's Palace, Estrada Monumental 139; www.belmond.com. Named after Reid's Scottish founder, this Michelin-starred hotel restaurant is formal but not starchy. Well-travelled Funchal-born chef José Diogo Costa works magic with the island's freshest ingredients, producing dishes to complement the panoramic coastal views. Three tasting menus, one of which is vegetarian. Evenings only. **€€€€**

Uva The Vine, Rua dos Aranhas 27; www.hotelthevine.com. Chic, contemporary venue for wine lovers, with showy dishes such as fish tartare with seaweed, roe and wasabi-scented avocado, topped with pansies. Evenings only. **€€€€**

Beyond Funchal

Adega do Pomar Quinta da Moscadinha, Rua Maria Ascensão, Camacha; www.quintadamoscadinha.com. This cosy, rustic restaurant serves beautifully cooked and presented traditional food in an old Madeiran tavern setting. It's on a small farm that rears hens and makes award-winning cider from hand-selected local apples. **€€€**

Arraial do Ribeiro Frio ER103 Estrada da Laurisilva 6, Ribeiro Frio. With the feel of a forest cabin, complete with wood fire (even in summer), this hospitable restaurant has a straightforward rural Madeiran menu featuring well-stuffed *bolo do caco* sandwiches, grilled meat and passionfruit dessert. **€€**

Caravela Avenida Macos Marques Rosa (ER101) 62, São Vicente. Seafront restaurant offering generous plates of locally sourced limpets, octopus and grilled fish with potatoes, rice and vegetables. The first-floor terrace has direct sea views. **€€**

Golden Calheta Avenida Dom Manuel I 10, Calheta; www.goldencalheta.com. All-day restaurant with a contemporary, international flavour, overlooking the marina. Brunch, a feast featuring granola, stuffed croissants or pancakes, rolls into lunch, which could be tapas, risotto or a luscious salad. **€€**

O Cesto Rua Maria Ascensão 93, Camacha. This simple, family-run restaurant celebrates seasonal produce with hearty, home-style cooking. The menu changes daily: expect filling bowls of *sopa de trigo* (wheat and vegetable soup), stewed beef with potatoes, or *dobrada* (tripe with beans). **€€**

Oxalis Casa Velha do Palheiro, Rua da Estalagem 23, São Gonçalo; www.casa-velha.com. Featured in the Michelin guide, this refined dining room in the grounds of the Quinta do Palheiro is one of the island's most elegant restaurants. Exquisite international and Portuguese dishes. Daily fixed-price and à la carte menus are available. Superb service and wine list. **€€€€**

Pipa Rua Dr. Abel de Freitas, Porto da Cruz. Casual restaurant near Porto da Cruz's beaches and lido, preparing delicious Madeiran seafood, such as juicy, garlicky limpets and grilled sardines, grouper or sea bream fillets with chips and salad. **€€**

Quinta do Furão Estrada da Quinta do Furão 6, Santana; www.quintadofurao.com. Upmarket vineyard restaurant in a rural hotel, set on a cliff with fine ocean and countryside views. The menu features contemporary-rustic fare such as grilled tuna, *espetadas* and *trigo* wheat with wild mushrooms, hazelnuts and cheese. **€€€**

Santo António Estrada João Gonçalves Zarco 656, Estreito de Câmara de Lobos; www.restaurantesantoantonio.com. In business since 1966, this churrascaria serves lusciously seasoned *espetadas*. For a truly authentic flavour, you can pay a little extra for a laurel skewer, rather than metal. **€€**

Porto Santo

Panorama Restaurant Estrada Carlos Pestana Vasconcelos, Casinhas; www.panorama-restaurante.pt. Set on a hilltop in one of the most fantastic spots on the island, wall-to-wall windows offer a stunning panoramic view of the entire island. From the kitchen come meat and fish dishes of great quality, such as grilled lamb chops in peppermint sauce or cod 'Panorama Style'. **€€€**

Rafaela Estrada Velha da Camacha 14, Camacha. This fabulous little contemporary café may look understated, but don't be fooled: it's run by a chef who trained at Funchal's Michelin-starred Il Gallo dOro. Every savoury snack and sweet treat is a mouthwatering work of art. **€**

Travel essentials

Practical information

Accessible travel

The newest hotels on Madeira have wheelchair-accessible rooms and adapted toilets, and museums and major sights are increasingly providing access ramps. However, narrow, cobbled pavements and hilly terrain can make getting from A to B a challenge.

Accessible taxis are available from **Aitram** (www.aitram.pt), but they vary in type, so spell out your requirements when requesting one. Removable ramps leading into the back of a van are more common than specially adapted vehicles with a lowered floor. Similarly, some (but not all) buses and coaches have low entrances and floors. Madeira's cable car, the Teleférico do Funchal, can carry one wheelchair per cabin; on request, it will slow down to allow people with reduced mobility to get on board.

Many of Madeira's classic hiking trails are unsuitable for people with disabilities. The exceptions include the PR9.1 JOEL path from Queimadas to Pico das Pedras, a 3.8km trail that's wheelchair-friendly and has handrails for the partially sighted, and the easy-going PR6.8 along Levada do Paul. An all-terrain wheelchair opens up more possibilities, such as the PR11 Vereda dos Balcões.

For advice, tours and equipment hire, contact **Disabled Accessible Travel** (www.disabledaccessibletravel.com), **Madeira Accessível by Wheelchair** (www.madeiraacessivelbywheelchair.pt), **Madeira Best** (www.madeira.best) and **TUR4all** (www.tur4all.com).

Accommodation (see also Camping)

The district with the most places to stay is Funchal's Zona Hoteleira (hotel zone), which hugs the coastal cliffs west of Funchal. It's home to grande dames such as Reid's Palace and luxurious resort hotels such as the Cliff Bay, the Royal Savoy and the Savoy Palace, along with more affordable, family-friendly options. Keen to shake off Madeira's old image as a staid destination, many have updated their design and services. Central Funchal has a smattering of small, characterful townhouse hotels and guesthouses *(pensões)* and elsewhere, the options are expanding, with boutique hotels and B&Bs popping up in low-key coastal, mountain and rural areas such as

Câmara de Lobos, Calheta, Ponta do Sol, Porto da Cruz and Santana.

Quintas, a Madeira speciality, are gracious mansions and villas, usually set in splendid gardens, brimming with antiques and restored to provide a standard of accommodation (and prices) equivalent to a four- or five-star hotel. While they may lack some of the facilities and amenities of a top resort hotel, they tend to offer more intimacy and character. It's best to book early.

Travellers familiar with Portugal might arrive on Madeira looking for a *pousada*, a luxury government-owned hotel set in a building of architectural and historical merit. Madeira only has one official *pousada*, Pestana Churchill Bay in Câmara de Lobos, but some quintas and other privately run hotels have a pousada-like ambience.

Virtually every area has self-catering **villas** and **apartments** available for rent, from basic studios and cottages to mini mansions with gardens and a pool. They offer more space for your money than a hotel room, with the added benefit of kitchen facilities, and some (such as the An Island Apart collection, www.anislandapart.com) are supremely stylish. A minimum rental period may apply. Package holiday deals can be great value.

In Portugal, peer-to-peer short-term rentals marketed through websites such as Airbnb and Booking.com are known as **Alojamento Local** (AL). They're increasingly common on Madeira and there's a concern that they're contributing to overtourism and housing shortages. As a rule, purpose-built pads are more community-friendly than accommodation that was originally intended for locals. As well as conventional flats and houses, quirky alternatives such as **glamping pods**, **tiny houses** and **yurts** are popping up in the countryside.

Wherever you choose to stay, early booking is recommended if you want to visit during the winter season between Christmas and New Year's Eve (see page 99).

I'd like a single/double room with bath/shower. **Queria um quarto simples/duplo com banho/chuveiro.**
What's the rate per night? **Qual é o preço por noite?**

Airports

Madeira's Aeroporto Internacional da Madeira Cristiano Ronaldo (www.aeroportomadeira.pt) is in Santa Cruz, 19km (12 miles) east of Funchal. It used to have one of the shortest passenger runways in Europe until it was enlarged in 2000. Even so, arriving is still an adventure, and occasionally, in really bad weather, flights have to be diverted to Porto Santo.

From the airport to Funchal it is about 35 minutes by taxi or up to an hour by the SIGA Aerobus (https://siga.madeira.gov.pt/aerobus), which stops near many of the city's hotels. During rush hour, double the time. Several car-hire agencies have desks at the airport, and there is a small tourist information kiosk, bureau de change, restaurant and bar.

There are daily flights from Madeira to **Porto Santo**'s tiny airport (www.aeroportoportosanto.pt) with Binter (www.bintercanarias.com). There are no airport buses, but taxis will drive you into Vila Baleira in under ten minutes.

Where can I get a taxi? **Onde posso encontrar um táxi?**
How much is it to central Funchal? **Quanto custa para ir ao centro de Funchal?**
Does this bus go to Funchal? **Vai para Funchal este autocarro?**

Apps

Bolt (www.bolt.eu), **Taxiin** (www.taxiin.pt), **Taxi-Link** (www.taxi-link.com) Taxis.

ProCiv Madeira (www.procivmadeira.pt) Emergency assistance from the Regional Civil Protection Service (IP-RAM). If you dial 112 via the app, IP-RAM's control centre receives your last known position and sends you real-time information concerning weather, fires and road closures.

SIGA (https://siga.madeira.gov.pt) Bus timetables and tickets (in development at the time of writing).

Bicycle hire

You can rent a mountain bike or e-bike from **Cycling Madeira** (www.

cyclingmadeira.com), **E-Bike Madeira** (www.ebikemadeira.com) or **Freeride** (www.freeridemadeira.com).

Budgeting for your trip

Getting to Madeira. There are regular scheduled and charter flights direct to Madeira (or via Lisbon) from many European cities. Return flights from London typically cost £125–350. Affordable package deals – flights and hotel included – are usually available.

Accommodation. Madeira's luxury hotels cost over €300 per room per night, with the top-end places charging more than €600. Mid-range places are good value at €150–300. Funchal also has a handful of places costing €50–150; there are more options in this price bracket in the rural areas.

Meals. Even top-rated restaurants may be surprisingly affordable compared to most European capitals. Portuguese wines are quite good and very attractively priced, even in fine restaurants. A three-course meal with wine in a reasonable establishment averages €25–50 per person. Many hotels offer half- and full-board plans.

Local transport. Buses and taxis are reasonably priced. Bus fares start at just over €1 per journey; hops within Funchal are €1.95, longer routes €2.60. Giro Passes (smartcards which act as monthly season tickets) and Giro Bilhetes (for occasional travel) cost less per hop.

Incidentals. Your other major expenses will be excursions, outdoor activities and entertainment. Hiring a car allows greater flexibility, assuming you're happy to contend with steep, challenging roads. Economy hire costs from €36–56 a day. Petrol costs around €1.76 a litre, and diesel is around €1.59. Coach trips from Funchal cost €20–40. Hopping to Porto Santo by air costs €90–160 return; by ferry, €56–68 return. Nightclub cover charges can be high, and folklore or fado shows, including dinner, run at €25–60 per person.

Camping

There's only one official campsite with facilities on Madeira, the Parque de Campismo de Porto Moniz (www.portomoniz.pt). There's also more than a dozen local government run wilderness campsites with minimal facilities, where you can pitch a tent for free. To do so, it's essential to book permits in advance via the Cultura e Lazer (Culture and Leisure) section of the Simplifica portal (https://simplifica.madeira.gov.pt), and to contact the local park rangers via the Instituto das Florestas e da Conservação da Natureza (https://ifcn.madeira.gov.pt) to say when you'll be arriving.

Is there a campsite near here? **Há algum parque de campismo por aqui perto?**
May we camp here? **Podemos acampar aqui?**

Car hire (see also Driving and Budgeting for your trip)

There are local and international car hire agencies in Funchal (most near the hotel and tourist zones) and at the airport. Prices vary significantly, so shop around – local firms tend to be cheaper and less prone to charging extra for scratches or dents.

You must be at least 21 and have held a valid national (or international) licence for at least a year. You need to present a valid credit card when booking. Third-party fire and theft is included in the basic charge. You'll need additional insurance, but you're not obliged to buy this from your rental agency: your credit card company or a specialist service such as Insurance4CarHire (www.insurance4carhire.com) may offer cover for less.

Major international agents include:
Avis (www.avis.com); **Europcar** (www.europcar.com); **Hertz** (www.hertz.pt); and **Sixt** (www.sixt.pt).

I'd like to hire a car **Queria alugar um carro**
… tomorrow **… para amanhã**
… for one day/one week. **… por um dia/uma semana.**
Please include full insurance. **Que inclua um seguro contra todos os riscos, por favor.**

Climate

Madeira is generally warm and spring-like all year, making it an excellent winter retreat for northern Europeans. However, winter months can be rather wet and windy. The rainiest period is from October to December, with an average of six to seven days of rain per month, but you can usually count on an average of six hours sunshine each day. From May to September, the air is warm and somewhat humid. The typical pattern, year-round, is a clear, bright morning, with clouds rolling down from the mountains in the afternoon. For warm, clear weather, ideal for mountain walking, summer is your best bet. Since the islands have multiple microclimates, it's a good idea to consult local webcams detailed weather apps such as Windy (www.windy.com) or Mountain Forecast (www.mountain-forecast.com) when planning excursions. Average daily temperatures are:

	J	F	M	A	M	J	J	A	S	O	N	D
min												
ºC	13	13	13	14	16	17	19	19	19	18	16	14
ºF	56	56	56	58	60	63	66	67	67	65	61	58
max												
ºC	19	18	19	19	21	22	24	24	24	23	22	19
ºF	66	65	66	67	69	72	75	76	76	74	71	67

Crime and safety (see also Emergencies and police)

Although Madeira is one of the safest places in the world for tourists, factors such as poverty (which does exist here, especially in small villages) inevitably make temptation irresistible for some, and there have been some problems with drug users mugging walkers along lonely *levada* trails. Follow the same general rules that you would elsewhere. Never leave anything of value in your car, even if it is out of sight. Burglaries of holiday accommodation are rare, but leave any valuables in a safe-deposit box, or, in a hotel, with reception staff. You must report any losses to the police within 24 hours and get a copy of your statement for insurance purposes.

I want to report a theft. **Quero participar um roubo.**

Driving

There are several reasons not to drive on Madeira: car hire and petrol are not cheap, but taxis are, and the mountain roads can be hard on one's nerves. Conversely, you may enjoy the challenge and, of course, a car gives maximum flexibility.

Road conditions. It is only worth considering driving into Funchal if you are staying well outside the town (at Machico or Garajau, for instance). If you do, expect traffic jams. The roads across the island offer a choice between fast modern highways, often enclosed in tunnels, or scenic but slow and winding mountain roads. The latter demand confident, relaxed drivers.

Rules and regulations. The rules are the same as in the rest of continental Europe: drive on the right, overtake on the left, and give way to vehicles coming from the right. Speed limits are 100–120kph (62–75mph) on highways, 90kph (56mph) outside built-up areas and 40–50kph (25–30mph) in built-up areas. Average speeds on country roads are well below 60kph (37mph). Seat belts must be worn at all times and children under the age of 12 are not allowed in front seats. Motorcyclists must always wear helmets.

Alto Stop
Cruzamento Crossroads
Curva perigosa Dangerous bend/curve
Descida íngreme Steep hill
Desvio Detour
Encruzilhada Crossing
Estacionamento permitido Parking permitted
Estacionamento proibido No parking
Guiar com cuidado Drive with care
Máquinas em manobras Men working
Obras/Trabalhos Men working

Paragem (de autocarro) Bus stop
Pare Stop
Pedestres, peões Pedestrians
Perigo Danger
Proibida a entrada No entry
Seguir pela direita/esquerda Keep right/left
Sem saída No through road
Are we on the right road for...? **É esta estrada para...?**
Fill it up, please, with... **Encha, por favor, de...**
three star/four star/unleaded/diesel **normal/super/sem chumbo/gasóleo**
My car's broken-down **O meu carro está avariado**
There's been an accident **H ouve um acidente**

If you need help. Car hire companies give out a number to contact in case of breakdown or emergency. If you belong to a motoring organisation affiliated to the **Automóvel Clube de Portugal** (www.acp.pt), you can use its services free of charge. You will have no problem finding well-equipped garages on Madeira.

Parking. Funchal has reasonably priced car parks at either end of town. Parking in the centre is virtually impossible, except in the 'blue zone' (metered parking) along Avenida do Mar, facing the Marina. You should have few difficulties parking elsewhere on the island. White lines signal free parking spaces and blue lines signal paid parking; yellow lines mean no parking.

Electricity

The standard current is 220-volt, 50Hz AC. For US appliances, 220v transformers and plug adaptors are needed.

I need an adaptor/a battery, please. **Preciso de um adaptador/uma pilha, por favor.**

Embassies and consulates

The following are located in Lisbon:

UK www.gov.uk/world/organisations/british-embassy-lisbon

Australia www.portugal.embassy.gov.au

Canada www.international.gc.ca/country-pays/portugal/lisbon-lisbonne.aspx

Republic of Ireland www.ireland.ie/en/portugal/lisbon

South Africa www.embaixada-africadosul.pt

US https://pt.usembassy.gov

> Where is the British embassy? **Onde é a embaixada inglesa?**

Emergencies (see also Health and medical care)

The emergency number for police, fire or ambulance is the same. Dial **112** for either service.

The nonprofit organisation Madeiran Sea Rescue Association (SANAS Madeira) is responsible for sea rescues. A Mountain Rescue Service is also available (dial the above number for both).

Hospital Dr Nélio Mendonça in Funchal (www.sesaram.pt) has a 24-hour emergency ward; tel: 291 705 606. Outside Funchal, ask for the local Centro de Saúde (Health Centre).

Getting there (see also Airports)

Air Travel. Madeira is served by frequent direct flights from international airports in London, the UK regions and all over Europe, all year round. There are also direct flights to Porto Santo from London Gatwick, Lisbon and Porto. The national Portuguese airline is TAP Air Portugal (www.flytap.com), which flies from several European cities to Funchal. Low-cost carriers include easyJet (www.easyjet.com), Jet2 (www.jet2.com) Ryanair (www.ryanair.com) and Tui (www.tui.co.uk). Inexpensive charter flights are also available. The flight time from London to Madeira is approximately 3 hours

30 minutes, and from Lisbon to Madeira about 1 hour 30 minutes.

Cruise liners stop off at the island, but often only for a brief tour.

Guides and tours (see Public transport)

A good way of seeing Madeira is by coach or minibus tour. Several operators go to the same places, but charge different rates for different services. Itineraries include: west of the Island; east of the Island, including Pico do Arieiro; a half-day covering Monte/Curral das Freiras/Pico dos Barcelos; guided *levada* walks; and Jeep safaris to out-of-the-way places such as Boca dos Namorados (see page 54) or Paúl da Serra (see page 59). Not all of these are good value; a trip to Monte is simple and inexpensive to do by yourself (see page 49), as are some *levada* walks (see page 70). Other options include a day trip to Porto Santo (only recommended in summer, when sunshine and calm sailing are the norm). Half-day boat trips cruise up and down the Madeiran coast, and other outings from Funchal Marina include a trip to the Ilhas Desertas, or a full day's sailing, including lunch and wine.

The tourist offices (see page 140) in Funchal – and most hotels – can provide information on local tour operators. Particularly highly recommended are **Lido Tours** (www.lido-tours.com), who offer small island minibus tours and *levada* and mountain walks, and **Windsor Travel** (www.windsormadeira.com), who run well-organised tours, including to the viewing point at Pico dos Barcelos and to Porto Santo.

Madeira Explorers (www.madeira-levada-walks.com) and **Nature Meetings** (www.naturemeetings.com) focus on guided outdoor ecotourism. **Hit the Road Madeira** (www.hittheroadmadeira.com) and **Up Mountain Madeira** organise ridge and *levada* walks and 4x4 adventures (www.upmountainmadeira.com).

We'd like an English-speaking guide/an English interpreter.
Queremos um guia que fale inglês/um intérprete de inglês.

Health and medical care (see also Emergencies)

There are numerous health centres on Madeira and one on Porto Santo. *Farmácias* (chemists) are open Monday to Friday 9am to 1pm, 3pm to 7pm, Saturdays 9am to 1pm. On the door of every pharmacy you will find postings of after-hours chemists.

Tourist offices carry lists of doctors and dentists who speak English. For more serious illness or injury, Hospital Dr Nélio Mendonça (Avenida Luis de Camoes 57; www.sesaram.pt) is the island's largest hospital and has English-speaking staff.

In an emergency, dial **112** for an ambulance.

It is highly recommended that you take out travel insurance to cover any costs associated with illness or accidents while abroad. EU and UK nationals with a European or Global Health Insurance Card (EHIC/GHIC), obtainable online at www.nhs.uk/using-the-nhs/healthcare-abroad, can receive free emergency treatment at Social Security and Municipal hospitals. Private hospitals are expensive. If you don't take the EHIC/GHIC with you, you must pay on the spot and claim on your travel insurance later. If you have an EHIC, you can continue to use it until it expires, after which you should apply for a GHIC as a replacement.

Where's the nearest (all night) pharmacy? **Onde fica a farmácia (de serviço) mais próxima?**
I need a doctor/dentist **Preciso de um médico/dentista**
an ambulance **uma ambulância**
hospital **hospital**
An upset stomach **Dôr de estômago**
Sunburn/a fever **Queimadura de sol/febre**

The most likely health problems will be due to an excess of sun or alcohol. Madeiran tap water (*água*) is safe and tastes pretty good. Bottled mineral water is sold everywhere.

Mosquitoes are present in summer, so use repellent or a plug-in device.

Holidays

1 January **Ano Novo** New Year's Day
Movable date, February **Terça-feira Gorda/Carnaval** Shrove Tuesday/Carnival
Movable date, March/April **Sexta-feira Santa** Good Friday
Movable date, March/April **Domingo de Páscoa** Easter Sunday
25 April **Dia da Liberdade** Freedom Day
1 May **Dia do Trabalho** Labour Day
10 June **Dia de Portugal** National Day
Movable date, June **Corpo de Cristo** Corpus Christi
1 July **Dia da Região Autónoma da Madeira e das Comunidades Madeirenses** Madeira Day
15 August **Assunção de Nossa Senhora** Feast of the Assumption
5 October **Dia da República** Republic Day
1 November **Dia de Todos os Santos** All Saints' Day
1 December **Dia da Restauração da Independência** Independence Restoration Day
8 December **Dia da Imaculada Conceição** Feast of the Immaculate Conception
25 December **Dia de Natal** Christmas Day
26 December **Dia de Santo Estêvão** St Stephen's Day (Boxing Day)

Language

Madeira's official language is Portuguese. Basic Spanish should help with reading signs and menus, but is unlikely to unlock the mysteries of spoken Portuguese.

The pocket-size *Rough Guides Phrasebook: Portuguese* covers most situations you are likely to encounter during a visit to Portugal.

LGBTQ+ travellers

Portugal's constitution is one of the few in the world to contain a ban on discrimination based on sexual orientation, and Portuguese lesbian, gay, bisexual, transgender, intersex, queer and asexual (LGBTQ+) rights are currently among the most advanced in the world. Madeira doesn't have any exclusively gay bars, clubs, hotels or beaches, but there's a good sprinkling of gay-friendly night spots in Funchal's Zona Velha.

Good day/afternoon/evening **Bom dia/Boa tarde/Boa noite**
Goodbye **Adeus**
please **faz favor/por favor**
thank you **obrigado/obrigada (male/female speaker**)
How do you do/Pleased to meet you **Muito prazer**
How are you? **Como está?**
Very well, thank you **Muito bem, obrigado/obrigada**
What does this mean? **Que quer dizer isto?**
Please write it down **Escreva-mo, por favor**
where/when/how? **onde/quando/como?**
how long/how far? **quanto tempo/a que distância?**
left/right **esquerdo/direito**
cheap/expensive **barato/caro**
hot/cold **quente/frio**
old/new **velho/novo**
open/closed **aberto/fechado**
vacant/occupied **livre/ocupado**
early/late **cedo/tarde**
Help me, please **Ajude-me, por favor**
day/week/month/year **dia/semana/mês/ano**
yesterday/today/tomorrow **ontem/hoje/amanhã**
Sunday **domingo**
Monday **segunda-feira**
Tuesday **terça-feira**
Wednesday **quarta-feira**
Thursday **quinta-feira**
Friday **sexta-feira**
Saturday **sábado**
What day is it today? **Que dia é hoje?**

Money (see also Budgeting for your trip)

Currency. The euro is the official currency used in Portugal. Notes are denominated in 5, 10, 20, 50, 100 and 500 euros; coins in 1 and 2 euros and 1, 2, 5, 10, 20 and 50 cents.

Currency exchange. While banks and the 24-hour bureau de change at the airport will exchange currency, for obtaining euros, ATMs are easiest and provide by far the best rates.

Credit cards. Standard international credit cards are widely accepted, except in some shops and restaurants, especially in small villages.

Can I pay with this credit card? **Posso pagar com cartão de crédito?**

I want to change some pounds/dollars. **Queria trocar libras/dólares.**

Can you cash a traveller's cheque? **Pode pagar um cheque de viagem?**

Where's the nearest bank/ currency exchange office? **Onde fica o banco mais próximo/a casa de câmbio mais próxima?**

How much is that? **Quanto custa isto?**

Opening hours

Most businesses close for a one- to two-hour lunch break. Shops and offices are generally open weekdays between 9am and 1pm and 3pm and 7pm, and from 9am to 1pm on Saturdays. Shopping centres and supermarkets open daily from 10am to 10pm. Banks are open between 8.30am and 3pm on weekdays, some also open on Saturdays between 9am–1pm. Currency exchange offices usually open between 9am and 1pm and 2pm and 7pm on weekdays, and until 1pm on Saturdays.

Museums are generally open Tuesday to Friday from 10am to 5pm, although some close between 12.30pm and 2pm, and some open at weekends, especially during summer. Café-restaurants may be open all day, whereas more up-market establishments tend to close after lunch and reopen for dinner.

Police (see also Emergencies)

The national police, identified by their blue uniforms, are generally helpful and friendly and often speak a little English. If you need assistance or find yourself in an emergency situation, dial 112. The main police station in Funchal, where there is a lost property section, is located on Rua da Infância 28 (www.psp.pt).

Where's the nearest police station? **Onde fica o posto de polícia mais próximo?**
I've lost… my wallet/bag/passport **Perdi... a minha carteira/o meu saco/o meu passaporte**

Public transport

Buses. Most of the island is served by public buses, which are cheap, reliable and generally punctual. With planning and patience, it is possible to go almost anywhere that coach tours visit by public bus, for a fraction of the cost. The tourist office sells a booklet giving details of bus services and routes. Bus stops are indicated by the sign *paragem*.

The SIGA bus network includes services run by three operators, CAM (https://siga.madeira.gov.pt), SIGA Rodoeste (www.rodoeste.com.pt) and Horários do Funchal (www.horariosdofunchal.pt). Funchal, the hub, doesn't have a bus station. Regular local buses connect Avenida do Mar in the centre to Estrada Monumental in the Zona Hoteleira, and Praia Formosa beyond. There are inter-urban bus stops on the seafront (on Avenida do Mar and near the Teléferico do Funchal cable car station) and on Estrada Monumental in the Zona Hoteleira. For route maps and timetables, visit https://siga.madeira.gov.pt.

You can pay per trip or, for discounted fares, buy a rechargeable Giro card from automatic machines around the city or from authorised sellers.

At the time of writing, SIGA plans to introduce a Giro app. Various charges apply, depending on the number of zones and days required. Children under six travel free and those aged 6–16 qualify for reduced fares.

Taxi. Metered taxis – found at ranks all over Funchal and in every town – are reasonably priced and convenient for most trips within Funchal and to sights just outside the city, such as Monte, the Jardim Botânico and the Quinta do Palheiro. For many popular tourist trips, there is a government-set flat fare, which, by law, has to be displayed inside the taxi. Otherwise, the meter begins at €3.50 (with a 20 percent surcharge between 9pm and 6am and on Sat, Sun and holidays). From the city centre to the hotel zone, expect to pay about €7. From the hotel zone to the airport costs around €25–35.

Many people hire taxis as substitutes for coach tours. If several people are travelling, this can be a good deal, since you'll be charged per car, not per person. A list of popular excursions and prices is kept at the tourist office, or see Taxi Madeira (www.taximadeira.com).

Cable car. The Teleférico do Funchal (www.madeiracablecar.com) connects Funchal's Zona Velha (Old Town) to Monte, in the mountains above the city, and takes approximately 15–20 minutes. There are several other cable cars dotted around the island.

Flights to Porto Santo. Porto Santo can be reached easily several times a day by small aircraft from Madeira airport (Binter; www.bintercanarias.com). Flight time approximately fifteen minutes, from about €90 return.

Ferry to Porto Santo. The Porto Santo Line (Avenida do Mar; www.portosantoline.pt) operates a cruise-style ferry that departs from Funchal's harbour daily at 8am, and takes about two hours. It leaves Porto Santo at 7pm and costs around €56–68 return. In winter the timetable is slightly reduced. The new ships are far more stable than the old but travel pills are recommended for anyone prone to seasickness.

Where is the nearest bus stop? **Onde é a paragem de autocarros mais próxima?**

When's the next bus to ...? **Quando parte o próximo autocarro para...?**
I want a ticket to ... **Queria um bilhete para**...
single/return **ida/ida e volta**
Will you tell me when to get off? **Pode dizer-me quando devo descer?**
Where can I get a taxi? **Onde posso encontrar um táxi?**
What's the fare to...? **Quanto custa um bilhete para...?**

Telephones

Portugal's country code is 351. Local numbers have nine digits with no leading zero; mobile numbers start with 9.

To make an international call, dial 00 for an international line plus the country code (eg UK 0044, US 001) plus phone number (including the area code, without the initial '0' where there is one).

Madeira has good mobile phone network coverage, and EU residents can 'roam like at home'. If you are travelling from outside the EU, check call and data charges with your mobile service provider before you go: if your phone is unlocked (which can be done locally), it's likely to be cheaper to obtain a Portuguese pay-as-you-go SIM card or e-SIM from local or international providers such as Airalo (www.airalo.com), MEO (www.meo.pt), NOS (www.nos.pt) or Vodafone (www.vodafone.pt).

My phone doesn't work here. **O meu telefone não funciona aqui.**

Time

Madeira operates both winter (GMT + 0) and summer (GMT + 1) time periods, so Madeira is on the same time as the UK. From the last Sunday in March until the last Sunday in October, the clocks are moved one hour ahead.

Times in summer are:

Sydney	**Madeira**	London	Los Angeles	New York
9pm	**noon**	noon	4am	7am

Tipping

As in mainland Portugal, gratuities are entirely optional. Hotel bills are generally inclusive, and taxi drivers do not expect a tip except for any special services. Locals only tip waiters and bar staff when they've received exceptional service. They do so by rounding up or leaving a few coins on the table: rarely more than 10 percent.

Toilets

Public toilets are rare on Madeira. The best place to find a clean toilet is in a large hotel, restaurant or bar (out of courtesy you should buy a drink, or at least ask permission). 'Ladies' is marked *Senhoras* and 'Gents' *Homens* or *Senhores*. Since the words *Senhoras* and *Senhores* are so similar, check carefully before entering. When hiking, carry a small bag for waste such as tissues, to avoid litter.

Where are the toilets please? **¿Por favor, onde é o quarto de banho?**

Tourist information

Portugal does not have national tourist offices as such. Instead it maintains a website, Visit Portugal (www.visitportugal.com), from which various brochures can be downloaded.

The Madeira Promotion Bureau has its own tourism website (www.visitmadeira.com) with plenty of information, and operates several offices in the archipelago. The most dependable are at the airport (daily 9am–9.30pm) and at Avenida Arriaga 16 in Funchal (Apr–Oct Mon–Fri

9am–8pm, Sat & Sun 9am–3.30pm; Nov–Mar Mon–Fri 9am–7pm, Sat & Sun 9am–3.30pm). Provincial offices in Ponto del Sol, Ribeira Brava, Porto Moniz, Santana and Porto Santo keep shorter hours.

Visas and entry requirements

Madeira is an autonomous region of Portugal, and are therefore part of the European Union. UK citizens, Americans, Canadians and many other nationalities do not need a visa to visit as a tourist, just a passport valid for six months. EU citizens may enter with an identity card. The length of stay authorised for most tourists is 90 days.

Before travelling to Madeira check official government websites or www.visitmadeira.com for updates.

Currency restrictions. Visitors from abroad may bring into Portugal (or depart with) any amount of euros or foreign currency.

Customs. Madeira is part of the EU, but has separate duty-free status within Portugal. Visitors from outside the EU can import the following amounts duty-free: 200 cigarettes, 50 cigars or 250g of tobacco; 1 litre of spirits; 4 litres of wine; 50g of perfume and 250ml of eau de toilette.

Websites

www.essential-madeira.com Local lifestyle magazine.

www.madeira-web.com Destination guide covering outdoor activities, island tours and events, plus live streaming from a network of webcams, dotted around the islands.

https://visit.funchal.pt Run by Funchal Town Hall, this official visitor guide to the city lists attractions, accommodation, restaurants and practicalities.

www.visitmadeira.com Official tourism board website for Madeira and Porto Santo, with lots of up-to-date information.

Index

MINI
MADEIRA

Second Edition 2025

Editor: Siobhan Warwicker
Author: Emma Gregg
Picture Manager: Tom Smyth
Cartography Update: Katie Bennett
Layout: Danielle Titmas
Production Operations Manager: Katie Bennett
Publishing Technology Manager: Rebeka Davies
Head of Publishing: Sarah Clark
Photography Credits: 123RF 7, 32, 61; Bigstock 56; Cliff Bay Hotel 20T; Dreamstime 14CR, 25, 42, 44, 65, 78, 79; Fotolia 10, 14TL, 15B, 37, 40, 58, 62, 66, 68, 77, 82, 90; iStock 15CB, 38, 54, 71, 86, 97, 105; Madeira Tourism 15CT, 35, 46, 52, 72, 84, 98; Madeira Tourism/Julio Marques 41; Orient-Express Hotels 107; Palheiro Nature Estate 48; Paul Murphy/Apa Publications 14BR; Phil Wood/Apa Publications 75; Public domain 23, 27, 28; Shutterstock 1, 8, 12, 14TR, 14CL, 14BL, 15T, 16T, 16CL, 16BL, 16BR, 18T, 18CL, 18BL, 18BR, 20CL, 20BL, 20BR, 30, 51, 80, 89, 92, 93, 95, 96, 101, 102, 103, 109, 110, 112, 114
Cover Credits: The coast at Seixal **Shutterstock**

About the author
Emma Gregg (www.emmagregg.com) is an award-winning, UK-based travel journalist who has visited all seven continents. She specialises in responsible tourism, ecotourism, nature, culture and islands. She particularly loves the Madeira Islands for their wild coastlines, mossy forests and sustainability-conscious spirit.

Distribution
UK, Ireland and Europe: Apa Publications (UK) Ltd; mail@roughguides.com
United States and Canada: Two Rivers; ips@ingramcontent.com
Australia and New Zealand: Woodslane; info@woodslane.com.au
Worldwide: Apa Publications (UK) Ltd; mail@roughguides.com

MIX
Paper from responsible sources
FSC® C014138

Special Sales, Content Licensing and CoPublishing
Rough Guides can be purchased in bulk quantities at discounted prices. We can create special editions, personalized jackets and corporate imprints tailored to your needs.
mail@roughguides.com
roughguides.com

EU Representative
LOGOS EUROPE, 9 rue Nicolas Poussin, 17000, LA ROCHELLE, France; Contact@logoseurope.eu; +33 (0) 667937378

Printed by Finidr in Czech Republic

ISBN: 9781835292440

This book was produced using **Typefi** automated publishing software.

A catalogue record for this book is available from the British Library

Contact us
Every effort has been made to ensure that this publication is accurate, free from safety risks, and provides accurate information. However, changes and errors are inevitable. The publisher is not responsible for any resulting loss, inconvenience, injury or safety concerns arising from the use of this book. If you notice any errors, outdated information, or potential safety risks, please send your comments with the subject line "Rough Guide Mini Madeira Update" to mail@roughguides.com.